An Anniversary to Remember

❦

YEARS ONE TO SEVENTY-FIVE

by
Cynthia Lueck Sowden

BRIGHTON PUBLICATIONS, INC.

BRIGHTON PUBLICATIONS, INC.

Brighton Publications, Inc.
PO Box 120706
St. Paul, MN 55112-0706
(612)636-2220

First Edition: 1992

Library of Congress Cataloging-in-Publication Data
Sowden, Cynthia Lueck
    An anniversary to Remember / by
Cynthia Lueck Sowden. — 1st ed.
        p. cm.
    Includes index.
    1. Wedding anniversaries.   2. Entertaining.   I. Title
GV1472.7.W38S67 1992
793.2 — dc20   92-7570
        ISBN 0-918420-17-2

Printed in the United States of America

To Grandma and Grandpa Anderson, who were married in 1923, and whose marriage is stronger than ever, and to Tom and Jean Henderson, who celebrated their Golden Wedding Anniversary in 1991. Both couples really know what love, marriage, and friendship are all about.

Special thanks to Warren and Joyce Kapsner, Rapid Graphics and Mailing, for sharing their wealth of resources and providing input and inspiration; and to Michael Macken, President, Macken Music and Entertainment Agency, whose imagination and experience added much to the anniversary music selections.

Contents

Introduction 15

Chapter 1: Celebrating Your Anniversary 17

    Anniversary Preparations at Your Wedding 18

    Etiquette 19

        Who Hosts the Party? 19

        Invitations 20

    Gifts 23

        Gifts to Each Other 23

        Gifts to the Anniversary Couple 24

        "No Gifts, Please" 24

        Monetary Gifts 25

        Card "Showers" 25

        Thank-yous 25

    Party Activities 26

    Decorations 27

    Music 28

    Programs 29

    Photos 29

    Publicity 30

    Reminding the Forgetful Spouse 31

    Remembering Widows and Widowers 32

Chapter 2: Anniversary One 33

    First Anniversary — Paper 34

Romantic Paper Picnic — 34

Videotape Viewing — 35

Paper Chase — 36

Attendants' Candlelight Dinner — 37

A Timely Celebration — 38

Gift Suggestions — 39

Gifts to Each Other — 40

Chapter 3: Anniversaries Two to Five — 41

Second Anniversary — Cotton — 42

Cotton Bowl Anniversary — 42

Harlem Cotton Club Anniversary Party — 43

Gift Suggestions — 44

Gifts to Each Other — 44

Third Anniversary — Leather — 45

American West — 45

Gift Suggestions — 46

Gifts to Each Other — 47

Fourth Anniversary — Flowers — 47

Floral Fantasy — 48

Gift Suggestions — 49

Gifts to Each Other — 49

Fifth Anniversary — Wood — 50

Tree-planting Ceremony — 50

Gift Suggestions — 51

Gifts to Each Other — 52

Chapter 4: Anniversaries Six to Ten — 53

Sixth Anniversary — Candy or Iron? — 54

The Sweet Sixth Anniversary — 54

Archaeological Dig — 55

Gift Suggestions — 56

Gifts to Each Other   57

Seventh Anniversary — Wool, Copper, Brass   57

    Reassessment Weekend   58

    Gift Suggestions   58

    Gifts to Each Other   59

Eighth Anniversary — Bronze   59

    Bronze Brunch   60

    Gift Suggestions   60

    Gifts to Each Other   61

Ninth Anniversary — Pottery or Willow   61

    Pottery Picnic   61

    Gift Suggestions   62

    Gifts to Each Other   62

Tenth Anniversary — Tin   63

    Tent Party   63

    Gift Suggestions   64

    Gifts to Each Other   64

Chapter 5: Anniversaries Eleven to Fifteen   65

Eleventh Anniversary — Steel   66

    Jamaican Steel Drum Party   66

    Gift Suggestions   67

    Gifts to Each Other   67

Twelfth Anniversary — Silk or Linen   68

    Arabian Nights Silken Fantasy   68

    Gift Suggestions   69

    Gifts to Each Other   69

Thirteenth Anniversary — Lace   70

    Victorian Lace Breakfast in Bed   70

    Wilkie Collins Moonstone Mystery Party   70

    Gift Suggestions   71

    Gifts to Each Other   72

Fourteenth Anniversary — Opal   72

     Australian Outback Barbecue   72

     Gift Suggestions   73

     Gifts to Each Other   74

Fifteenth Anniversary — Crystal   74

     Cinderella's Crystal Ball   74

     Gift Suggestions   75

     Gifts to Each Other   76

Chapter 6: Anniversaries Sixteen to Twenty   77

Sixteenth Anniversary — Topaz   78

     South American Sampler   78

     Gift Suggestions   79

     Gifts to Each Other   79

Seventeenth Anniversary — Amethyst   80

     Grecian Holiday   80

     Gift Suggestions   81

     Gifts to Each Other   81

Eighteenth Anniversary — Garnet   81

     Victorian Romance   82

     Gift Suggestions   82

     Gifts to Each Other   82

Nineteenth Anniversary — Aquamarine   83

     Seashore Holiday   83

     Gift Suggestions   84

     Gifts to Each Other   84

Twentieth Anniversary — China   84

     Chinese Garden Party   85

     Roaring Twenties Twentieth   85

     Gift Suggestions   86

     Gifts to Each Other   87

Chapter 7: Anniversary Twenty-five   89

    Twenty-fifth Anniversary — Silver   90

        Traditional Silver Jubilee   90

        "Come as You Were 25 Years Ago" Party   91

        Ethnic Anniversary Celebration   92

        Twenty-fifth Reaffirmation   94

        Gift Suggestions   95

        Gifts to Each Other   95

Chapter 8: Anniversaries Thirty, Thirty-five, Forty,
    Forty-five   97

    Thirtieth Anniversary — Pearl   98

        Medieval Madness   98

        Gift Suggestions   99

        Gifts to Each Other   99

    Thirty-fifth Anniversary — Coral   100

        Great Couples   100

        Gift Suggestions   101

        Gifts to Each Other   102

    Fortieth Anniversary — Ruby   102

        Ruby-colored Fortieth   102

        Gift Suggestions   104

        Gifts to Each Other   104

    Forty-fifth Anniversary — Sapphire   104

        Hawaiian Sapphire Celebration   105

        Gift Suggestions   106

        Gifts to Each Other   106

Chapter 9: Anniversary Fifty   107

    Fiftieth Wedding Anniversary — Gold   108

        Golden Anniversary Gala   108

        Fiftieth Family Reunion   109

"Fifties" Fiftieth Anniversary   111
    Gift Suggestions   112
    Gifts to Each Other   113

Chapter 10: Anniversaries Fifty-five, Sixty,
    Seventy-five   115
    Fifty-fifth Anniversary — Emerald   116
        Emerald City Party   116
        Gift Suggestions   117
        Gifts to Each Other   117
    Sixtieth Anniversary — Diamond   118
        Sixtieth Diamond Jubilee   118
        Gift Suggestions   119
        Gifts to Each Other   119
    Seventy-fifth Anniversary — Platinum   120
        Platinum Anniversary Party   120
        Gift Suggestions   122
        Gifts to Each Other   122

Chapter 11: Great Dates: Anniversary Celebrations
    for Just the Two of You   123
    Anniversary High Tea   124
    Artful Afternoon   124
    Business . . . or Pleasure?   125
    Champagne Balloon Flight   125
    Classic Camp-out   126
    Dancing in the Dark   127
    Dinner Theatre Date   128
    The Kidnaped Bride/Groom   128
    Log Cabin Anniversary   129
    Love in the Morning   130
    Luxurious Limo Ride   131

Moonlight on Horseback   131

Movie Date   131

Riverboat Romance   132

Romantic VCR Retreat   133

Second Honeymoon   134

Silent Celebration   135

Sports Night Out   135

Suites for the Sweet   136

Tandem Treat   137

A Way to a Man's (or Woman's!) Heart   137

Chapter 12: Anniversary Symbols   139

Chapter 13: Flowers That Say "I Love You"   145

Index   153

About the Author   159

Introduction

The idea for this book came to me as I was researching my first manuscript, *Wedding Occasions: 101 New Party Themes for Wedding Showers, Rehearsal Dinners, Engagement Parties, and More*! (Brighton Publications, 1990). I was browsing through the card catalog at the public library, and I noticed only one entry for "wedding anniversaries." Curious, I flipped to the "A" microfiche and looked under "anniversaries, wedding." Only two books were listed: the one I had found under the "wedding" listing, and one other. Its language reflected racial and gender stereotypes that made it hopelessly dated, and it contained themes and ideas which did not reflect the tremendous resources available to us now which make our parties fun and interesting. Nevertheless, these two books and a list of anniversary symbols from Hallmark Cards were the jumping-off point for this book.

My own fascination with anniversaries began with a book given to me by my maternal grandmother. Published in 1900, *Twentieth Century Etiquette* is a quaint, charming book lavishly illustrated with pictures of women in small-waisted dresses with leg o'mutton sleeves. It gives "rules for conduct in public, social, and private life, at home and abroad," including detailed instructions for riding a bicycle in a lady-like manner, and the proper way to leave behind one's calling card. It also contains a list of the symbols of wedding anniversaries, and some of the social rules for celebrating them.

Antiquated as it is, my husband and I refer to this book's anniversary list each October when our anniversary rolls around. We use the year's symbol as a guide to finding each other a suitable anniversary present.

This book was written with two distinct audiences in mind: couples seeking new and different ways to celebrate their anniversaries; and family members who suddenly find themselves in the position of planning a special anniversary such as a Silver or Golden wedding anniversary party. While many of the themes can be followed to the letter, this book is really meant to act as a springboard for your own exciting, creative anniversary celebrations.

One final note: Much of the first draft of this book was written in longhand on ruled notebook paper while I sat on the dock of our summer home. Ralph and I made the down payment on two and a half wooded acres there on our fifth (Wood) anniversary. It's the best anniversary gift we've ever given each other.

Enjoy the book, and enjoy your marriage. And may you have many happy anniversaries to come.

Celebrating
Your Anniversary

C elebrating your anniversary, whether publicly or privately, is an annual renewal of your commitment to each other. It's the one day each year you take time out for just the two of you. It's a day to rediscover why you fell in love in the first place!

It's easy, in our rushed society, to forget important days such as birthdays and anniversaries. Do not let your anniversary pass unnoticed. If you cannot celebrate on the exact date, make a point of celebrating *near* it. Your wedding day celebrated the beginning of your marriage; your anniversary celebrates its continuation.

Anniversary Preparations at Your Wedding ____

Believe it or not, the time to think about your first wedding anniversary is when you're preparing for your wedding. Be aware of little things you can do during your wedding or items that you can save for use on your anniversary celebrations in the years ahead. For instance:

• Save the top layer of your wedding cake, and share it on your first anniversary. Wrap the cake in plastic wrap and several layers of aluminum foil and store it in a self-sealing plastic bag in your freezer. Remove the cake from the freezer and allow it to thaw for several hours before serving. (Note: This works well if the top layer is made of fruitcake. Other types of cake — especially those with butter in the frosting — may not keep as well. Consider eating it on your one-month anniversary instead!)

• Collect all the candles used during the wedding ceremony and melt them down into one large candle which you and your loved one can light each year on your anniversary.

• Hire a professional videographer to videotape your wedding. Have it edited (most wedding videos are *way* too long!), then play it back on your anniversary.

• Many brides carry one bouquet for the ceremony and toss a smaller version at the reception. If you saved your wedding bouquet, use it as a dried centerpiece at a romantic anniversary dinner for two, as in "Fourth Anniversary Floral Fantasy." Or order a dried bouquet to carry and keep.

• No doubt you've purchased an album full of wedding photos from your photographer. When you pick up your completed album from the studio, why not make an appointment for an anniversary portrait?

• If you use paper napkins imprinted with your names and the wedding date when you serve punch or cake at your reception, save the unused napkins. Take them with you the following year on a "Romantic Paper Picnic."

• For a wedding gift, the groom may wish to present the bride with a necklace or bracelet to which a pearl or diamond can be added at each anniversary.

• If ribbons and lace were used as pew markers at the wedding ceremony, gather them up and make lacy pillow tops. They'll be the perfect cushion for your thirteenth anniversary "Victorian Lace Breakfast in Bed!"

• If embroidery is one of your favorite pastimes, spread a new, plain white tablecloth on the guest book table at your reception. As guests sign in, ask them to autograph the tablecloth as well. (Provide a fabric marker, available at craft and fabric stores, for signatures.) After the wedding, work the signatures in white pearle embroidery floss. Who knows, maybe you'll have it done in time for your Linen (twelfth) Anniversary!

• By all means, save your wedding gown. Imagine the thrill it'll cause when you wear it at your Seventy-fifth Anniversary!

Etiquette

Many couples prefer to celebrate by themselves, or informally with friends. Indeed, many of the early anniversaries are celebrated only by the couple. Some anniversaries, however, demand special attention. These are the more formal celebrations at 15, 20, 25, 50, 60 and 75 years.

As with weddings, there are do's and don't's for wedding anniversaries.

Who Hosts the Party?

As a rule, couples give their own anniversary parties in the early years of the marriage. This does not, however, preclude their friends or relatives from throwing a party for them.

Couples may also give their own anniversary parties for the "big" anniversaries such as 25 and 50. Usually, however, this duty is taken over by their children, or by siblings or close friends if the couple has no children.

If you will be hosting a party for the couple, be sure to respect their wishes. If they prefer not to receive gifts, do not make gift-giving a highlight of the celebration. If they do not react well to sudden changes of plan, or prefer intimate, well-planned affairs, don't spring a surprise party on them. If, on the other hand, they're a spontaneous couple who are up for any kind of adventure, line up the members of your *gang*, lure the couple to a party destination and yell, "Surprise!"

Invitations

People are busy these days with careers, home, and family. Give them plenty of time to place your anniversary celebration on their social calendar by issuing invitations four to six weeks in advance.

Invitations to early anniversary celebrations can be made through informal telephone calls or preprinted, fill-in-the-blank cards that are easily obtained from stationery stores. You can also issue invitations through hand-written notes, such as:

> Dear Marie and John,
>
> We're having a silver wedding anniversary for my parents on Saturday, October 12, at the Red Lion Restaurant. The party will begin at 8:00 P.M. I hope you can join us.
>
> Sincerely,
>
> Ed

If you are hosting your own anniversary party, you may want to send an invitation such as this:

> Dear Dean and Shirley,
>
> Please join us to celebrate our anniversary with a small dinner party at our home on Saturday, June 15 at 7:00 P.M.
>
> Love,
>
> Sally and David

If you have the time, you can make your own invitations. Suggestions for make-your-own invitations are sprinkled throughout the book.

Here's an example of an informal invitation offered by a wedding stationery supplier:

> Because you play a special part
> in our lives, we invite you
> to celebrate with us 10 years of
> sharing, caring, and loving each other.
> Dinner will be served
> with dancing to follow on Saturday, the twenty-second of August
> at six o'clock in the evening
> Holiday Inn Downtown
> St. Paul, Minnesota
> Linda and Steve

More formal invitations are used for a twenty-fifth or fiftieth anniversary celebration. Silver anniversary invitations are often engraved and printed in silver; fiftieth, in gold. These invitations can be obtained through any printer who does wedding invitations.

Some common forms of formal invitations include the following:

1941 — 1991
The Children of
Anne and Randall White
request the honor of your presence
at the
Fiftieth Anniversary
of the marriage of their parents
on Saturday, the tenth of August
nineteen hundred and ninety-one
at eight o'clock
Regency Hotel
Marion, Ohio

If the couple issues the invitation themselves, it could read:

1970 — 1995
Mr. and Mrs. Avery Townsend
request the pleasure of your company
at a reception
in honor of
their silver wedding anniversary
Saturday, the first of February
at eight o'clock
Golden Valley Country Club
Denver, Colorado

If the couple is more informal, you may wish to use the wording provided by a stationery supplier. The first is for use by a couple who are giving their own party; the second is for children of the couple.

Forty years have come and gone
through fair and stormy weather
We feel it's time to celebrate
because we're still together
So with great joy we anticipate
that you will keep this dinner date
on Saturday the eighth of August
at five o'clock in the afternoon
Waterbury Country Club
Fort Worth, Texas
Lauren and Tom

Now days it's strange to see
a marriage such as this
One that spans twenty-five years
of wonderful wedding bliss
We the offspring of that union,
to show that they are dear
Are having a party for them
to celebrate this special year.
Given by Mary, Susan and Paul
In honor of: Jim and Carol Morris
Date: August 13
Time: 5:00 p.m.
Place: 626 Fourth Avenue south
Rochester, New York

Although these invitations are usually engraved, you can give yours a more personal touch. Use calligraphy to create an original invitation (use black ink for better reproduction). Then have it printed on wedding stationery. Choose the ink color most suited to the occasion — silver for a twenty-fifth anniversary, metallic red for a fortieth (ruby) or metallic green for a fifty-fifth (emerald) anniversary, or gold for a fiftieth. Use matching inks to address the mailing envelopes.

When you address invitations, follow the same procedures as for a wedding invitation. On the outside of envelope, write the names of the persons you are inviting, such as "Mr. and Mrs. Kenneth Johnson," or "Mr. Roger Olson." On the inside envelope, write "Kenneth and Maryann" or "Roger and guest." If you are inviting children, be sure to list their names on the inside envelope. If their names aren't listed, they are not invited.

Invitations may also be issued via an announcement in the local newspaper or church bulletin:

Open House
to celebrate the forty-fifth anniversary
of Mr. and Mrs. Bradley Clinton
Sunday, April 21, 4 to 6 p.m.
United Methodist Church

A reaffirmation ceremony sometimes is included in the anniversary activities. Although a reaffirmation can be made in any year, many couples like to renew their vows at their twenty-fifth or fiftieth anniversaries. An invitation to a reaffirmation may be worded like this:

A life of sharing, caring
A love of endless giving together
The honor of your presence is requested
at the reaffirmation of wedding vows of
Mr. and Mrs. John Garvey
on Saturday, the seventh of November
Nineteen hundred and ninety-two
at four o'clock in the afternoon
Bethany Lutheran Church
Minneapolis, Minnesota

Gifts

Gifts to Each Other

Anniversary gift-giving is not required. However, it is a nice way to remember your special day — and to keep the romance in your marriage.

Some couples give each other a gift they can share or use together. These, too, should have some special meaning. Although practical gifts are nice, is anyone really thrilled by a new washer? When you shop for an anniversary gift, look for something appropriate to the occasion.

At the end of each party-theme chapter in this book is a list of gift suggestions for each anniversary covered in that chapter. It's not necessary to follow the themes, but matching a gift to an anniversary symbol can make the gift more fun and memorable. The hunt for the right gift is part of the fun!

Gifts to the Anniversary Couple

Anniversary parties are often gift-giving occasions, although guests aren't specifically required to bring gifts to the party. At the end of each of the party-theme chapters in this book are suggestions for gifts for the anniversary couple.

Card and gift shops often carry items for anniversaries. They range from commemorative plates to picture frames. Jewelers sometimes carry these items, too. To make these gifts more meaningful (and to take away some of their mass-produced flavor), have the names of the anniversary couple painted or engraved on the gift.

"No Gifts, Please"

Etiquette experts are divided on gift-giving to the anniversary couple, especially when the couple does not wish to be presented with gifts.

Some people put the phrase, "No gifts, please" on the anniversary invitation. Judith Martin, author of *Miss Manners' Guide for the Turn-of-the-Millennium*, finds this offensive, and says the phrase implies that gifts are expected. Marjabelle Young Stewart, author of *The New Etiquette*, says an invitation to an anniversary party *obliges* the guest to bring a gift, unless otherwise stated.

Elizabeth L. Post, author of *Emily Post's Etiquette*, says the request should be honored.

Perhaps the best way to say "No Gifts" comes from advice columnist Ann Landers:

No gifts, please. Your presence will be our cherished gift, and we respectfully request no other.

If you wish to do something for society, you may wish to follow the lead of Eleanor Burley, Sterling Heights, Michigan, who sent the following invitation to "Dear Abby:"

Your love and friendship is the only gift we need. However, if you wish to bring something, please make it an item of food that will be donated to the needy.

Mrs. Burley and her husband took ten boxes of canned goods and $200 in cash to the local food shelf.

Monetary Gifts

Gifts of money may not appear to be as thoughtful as a gift that has been shopped for carefully, or made expressly for the couple by the giver. In some instances, however, money may be the best gift of all. An elderly couple living on a fixed income will likely find money more useful than a sterling silver tea service.

A "Money Tree" is an attractive way of presenting a monetary gift. Roll up bills or checks and tape them to an artificial tree or a dry branch. Or wrap silver dollars in plastic wrap and tie the "fruit" to the tree with ribbon. Gift certificates from the couple's favorite department store would be a useful alternative.

Under no circumstances should you solicit money from guests. Even though you and your siblings may be planning to send Mom and Dad on a trip to Europe, you should not ask guests to help you pay for the airfare. However, if, after receiving an invitation to the party, a guest calls you and asks what gifts would be appropriate, you can tell him or her about your plans. The guest can then decide if he or she wants to contribute to the trip, or to give gifts that would be handy for travelers, such as luggage or an electrical voltage converter for hair dryers and electric shavers.

Card "Showers"

Some couples don't want a lot of hoopla on their anniversaries, even the "major" ones. Others may have moved to a retirement home in another state, far from old friends and relatives. One way to remember their special day is to hold a card shower. Mention of the shower can be included in a news release to the local newspaper, or you can mail a separate notice to the couple's friends.

A simple postcard works best. Address one side as usual. On the other side, write, "The 16th of May marks the 50th Anniversary of Howard and Mary Huston. Please help them celebrate! The love and thoughts of family and friends mean a lot to them. A card or call from you on this special day would make this an even more special occasion." Be sure to include the couple's address and telephone number.

Thank-yous

Surprisingly, some etiquette experts are kind to anniversary couples when it comes to thanking guests for their anniversary gifts, allowing them to voice a simple "thank-you" at the end of the party

Wedding stationers offer a couple of alternatives. One is a printed scroll which can be arranged at dinner or buffet settings or handed to guests as they leave. Following is a sample of such a scroll:

> This is only a tiny message,
> But it's written just for you
> Who found time in your busy life
> To give us a moment or two
> We hope that you can feel
> As we, lighthearted and gay,
> And share with us the magic,
> Of this enchanting day.
> Mr. and Mrs. Tom Smith

The scrolls can be bound with ribbons, or with imitation gold or silver wedding bands.

Another alternative is the photo thank-you. Take a copy of the couple's original wedding photo and a current portrait to the wedding stationer, who prints them in a folded thank-you note. Often, the verse runs like this:

> THANK YOU
> Friends and neighbors
> And relatives so dear,
> For all the joys you've wished us,
> And for your presence here.
> Now when this day is over,
> And our guests are on their way,
> The memory of this joyous time
> Will ever with us stay
> Mike and Leone

And, of course, there's the tried-and-true method of handwritten thank-you notes to each guest. A personal message is always in good taste.

Party Activities

Many of the party themes in this book are offered as suggestions for the married couple who wish to invite their friends to help them celebrate their anniversary, or for friends or relatives who wish to give a party for the anniversary pair. The party themes and the suggested activities are only suggestions; they need not be followed to the letter.

There are some activities which probably should be part of any large anniversary party.

One is a receiving line. As they did at their wedding reception, the couple stand near the door and greet guests. They may be joined by their children. If the party is hosted by someone else, the host or hostess is also part of the receiving line. If the couple is elderly and cannot stand for long periods of time, they may be seated in a place of honor, and the guests file past to offer their congratulations.

Toasts are another common feature of anniversary celebrations. They may be given by the best man, or by one of the couple's children. Toasts should be simple and to the point — "To Wally and Alice. After 60 years, their love is still strong." or, "To Dick and Delores. May their marriage continue for another 40 years!"

Gifts can be a nettlesome feature of anniversary parties. Let the couple decide if they will open gifts at the party, or open them later in private. If the gifts are opened at the party, one of the couple's children or a close friend should be appointed to make a list of the gifts.

Decorations

Decorations make any party room more festive. The celebration themes in this book offer several suggestions for setting the right mood.

Party decorations of almost any description are available at specialty shops. You'll find napkins and tablecloths, paper plates, streamers, banners that proclaim "Happy Anniversary" in silver or gold, honeycomb tissue-paper bells, and balloons.

If you'd like decorations imprinted with the names of the anniversary couple, shop the anniversary section of a bridal stationery book. There you'll find cake tops, matchbooks, ashtrays, cake servers, champagne glasses (for anniversary toasts), guest books, anniversary candles with stick-on numbers, and video cases for storing anniversary videos, as well as plates, cups, napkins, and tablecloths.

As with a wedding, flowers are an important decorative element. For twenty-fifth anniversaries, white flowers are the color of choice, while the fiftieth calls for gold or yellow flowers.

At any anniversary party, you'll want to have a place of honor reserved for the couple to receive their guests. If it's a formal dinner, have a head table set up for them. Seated next to them at the table would be the best man and the maid of honor (if they are present), and their spouses. The couple's children would also be seated at the head table, with the oldest son on his mother's right and the oldest daughter on the father's left.

Music

Life without music would be incomplete; the same is true of an anniversary celebration.

Typically, anniversary celebrations are smaller parties than traditional wedding receptions. Because of this, couples (or their party-givers) often choose live musicians to perform at an anniversary. If, however, you are having a large party (such as "Cinderella's Crystal Ball"), you may want to hire a disc jockey.

Trios of strolling musicians are also popular anniversary choices. Instrumentation can include a violin, accordion, or upright bass. A guitarist is sometimes substituted for an accordionist. Solo pianists or harpists add a distinct note of elegance.

Anniversaries are sentimental occasions. Therefore, songs that hold a special meaning to the anniversary couple should be included. For instance, if the couple was married or honeymooned in San Francisco, be sure to ask the musicians to play, "I Left My Heart in San Francisco."

Music should also be geared to the tastes of the anniversary couple. For instance, if they enjoy dancing polkas and schottisches, then an Old Time music trio — accordion, drums, and saxophone — is in order. If the couple was married during World War II, during the Big Band era, they'll appreciate hearing "Moonlight Serenade" or "I'm Gettin' Sentimental Over You" from a sax, piano, and drums trio. A couple married in the 1960s might enjoy listening to Beatles music once more.

And don't forget the "traditional" anniversary tunes:

"Anniversary Song," by Al Jolson and Saul Chaplin; "Anniversary Waltz," by Al Dugan and Dave Franklin; "When I Grow Too Old To Dream," by Oscar Hammerstein II and Sigmund Romberg; and "Silver Threads Among the Gold," by E.E. Rexford and H.P. Danks.

Other musical suggestions are scattered among the themes in this book.

Programs

Printed programs add a nice touch to a large, formal anniversary celebration or reaffirmation ceremony. Much like the programs so popular at wedding ceremonies, the anniversary programs list the sequence of events and prominent players in the day's activities.

Program covers can be obtained at a wedding stationer's, or, if the anniversary will be held at the couple's church or synagogue, from the house of worship. Printers who deal in wedding invitations also carry covers.

The information to be printed inside can be typeset by the printer. Or, if you know a good calligrapher, the program can be hand lettered. The printer will make a printing plate from the original artwork.

In addition to listing the names of the participants and the order of the ceremony or party activities, the program can also include a brief paragraph summarizing the history of the couple's marriage. The names of the original wedding party members can be listed, and marriage highlights such as the birth dates of the couple's children or a move from one city to another can be described.

Photos of the couple on their wedding day and as they are today may be printed inside or on the cover of the program.

Photos

By all means, take photographs at your anniversary celebrations — they're a wonderful way to capture treasured moments.

On "special" anniversaries such as the twenty-fifth, consider hiring a professional photographer to catch all the action. These anniversaries provide a wonderful opportunity to take family portraits, too, when the clan is gathered for the occasion.

You may want to arrange for a sitting at the photographer's studio for a new portrait of the two of you. Paired in a double frame with your original wedding portrait, it makes a priceless keepsake for succeeding generations.

Photos make great anniversary gifts, too — especially if they're presented in an anniversary album. Photos of the couple collected over the years of their marriage not only preserve precious memories, but give future generations a glimpse at their lives as well.

Publicity

Most wedding anniversaries are observed without much fanfare. However, milestone anniversaries such as the Twenty-fifth and Fiftieth are often announced in the local newspaper.

Although many big-city dailies have discontinued printing such notices, neighborhood and small-town weeklies still carry them. The amount of space devoted to such articles depends on the newspaper's circulation and frequency. Typically, the smaller the paper, the longer the article.

Send a short news release in advance of the event (at least a week).

Use the following format:

> John and Janice Brereton will celebrate their Silver Wedding Anniversary Sunday, September 10. An open house will be held in their honor from 2:00 P.M. to 5:00 P.M. at Calvary Baptist Church. The party will be hosted by the couple's children and grandchildren. Let your presence be your gift.

If the couple will be celebrating privately, but still wants the world to know about the anniversary, you can use this format:

> Fritz and Lydia Schmidt of Worthington will celebrate their 60th anniversary Sunday with a family dinner at the Holiday Inn. Their guests will be their immediate family members. The couple's children have requested a card shower. Cards should be sent to 555 Jackson Street, Little Rock, Iowa.

If possible, include a photo of the couple with the news release. Black-and-white photos still give the best reproduction. Write their names on the back of the picture with a special photo marker (available at photography stores and at some photo-processing outlets), or with a china marker. Do *not* use ballpoint pen (it will make indentations on the photo) or a felt-tip pen (the ink may smudge or bleed through the photo). Sandwich the picture between two pieces of cardboard and tape the cardboard shut. This will keep it from getting damaged in the mail.

Be sure to clip any notices that are printed, and put them in a scrapbook for the couple, along with photos and other memorabilia.

Reminding the Forgetful Spouse _____

Caught up in the busy whirl of day-to-day activities, even the most thoughtful persons can sometimes forget a birthday or anniversary. A little reminder never hurt anyone. If you're sentimentally inclined and your spouse is not, and you want to be remembered on your anniversary, don't take anything for granted. Take the initiative. Be ready to remind him (or her) that your anniversary is coming.

Many people hang a calendar in the kitchen, near the telephone, to record doctors' and dentists' appointments, concert dates, dinner invitations, and the like. Take a red marker, and in big letters, write, "Happy Anniversary" on your anniversary date. Circle it, too.

Or, purchase an appointment book and give it as a birthday gift or at Christmas. Circle your anniversary date, and write your name in the appropriate appointment slot, next to lunch or dinner.

If you draw the forgetful one into planning an activity, he'll be less likely to forget. Approach it lightly, saying, "Honey, our anniversary is coming up in two weeks. Let's do something special." Then plan a weekend getaway or a night on the town.

If your spouse listens to a certain radio station at home or at work, call the station's request line and ask that a certain, special song be played. Have it dedicated to "Alex and Dawn, on their tenth wedding anniversary." Or sponsor a program on a public radio station in honor of your anniversary.

Take advantage of new technology. Send a fax to your loved one with a simple message such as "Dinner reservations at Giorgio's, 7:00 P.M. tonight. Happy Anniversary!"

You can also send flowers to the office with a card that says, "I love you! Happy Anniversary!" Attention from co-workers who crowd around to see the flowers and ask who sent them will surely spark a memory. Or send a singing telegram that expresses your love (and gets the message across) in unforgettable (but tasteful) fashion.

If subtle messages don't work, rent a billboard for a week. (Sure, it's expensive, but desperate times call for desperate measures!) Buy space on a billboard that's located on the way to or from work, and advertise your love — and your anniversary — for all the world to see.

Remembering Widows and Widowers _____

Some people are super-organized, and they remember every birthday and anniversary with a card. If you're one of those persons, bless you. You really know how to brighten someone's day. But what do you do when one of the marriage partners dies?

An anniversary card to the surviving spouse can border on tactlessness — especially if the partner's death was quite recent.

Much depends upon the surviving spouse. Some people prefer to have their anniversaries remembered this way. Others definitely do not.

If you think your friend will appreciate an anniversary card, by all means, send one. If, however, you're not sure how an anniversary card would be received and you want to remember the widow or widower on the anniversary date, do so with a "Thinking of You" card, or by taking her or him out for a quiet dinner. The expression of friendship will be appreciated, and you won't dredge up any painful memories.

Anniversary
One

Your first anniversary is special. It's the first of many celebrations that commemorate your wedding day. It also marks the passage of time, and the end of a period of adjustment. During the past year, you've become accustomed to one another, to your new home, your new families. Your commitment to each other has deepened.

First anniversary celebrations are typically rather quiet. You may choose to celebrate by yourselves, or with your parents or your wedding attendants. These people may host a party for you, or you may invite them to your home. Whatever the size of the guest list, the occasion demands simplicity.

First Anniversary —

Paper

Even in this age of high-tech electronics, we still commit our most important documents — such as marriage licenses — to paper. Like fine-quality paper, marriage is delicate. Paper perfectly symbolizes the delicate relationship of the first year of marriage.

Romantic Paper Picnic _____

A picnic for two under a shady tree or on a sunny hillside covered with wildflowers provides a properly romantic setting for your first anniversary celebration. If you married in winter, don't despair. If your area boasts cross-country ski trails, you can ski to a local park and hold an impromptu cookout. Or spread a paper tablecloth on your living room floor.

Your tablecloth, napkins, plates, and cups should all be made of paper for this occasion — in your wedding colors, of course! (If you have napkins imprinted with your names and your wedding date leftover from your wedding, today's a great day to use them!) Tote your picnic accessories to the picnic site in a wicker basket. When your party is over, simply roll the dirty dishes up in the table cloth and dispose of the entire mess in a nearby trash container.

Perhaps the most famous romantic picnic menu ever was described in the *Rubaiyat of Omar Khayyam* — "a Loaf of Bread beneath the Bough, a Flask of Wine, a Book of Verse — and Thou beside me singing in the Wilderness". You and your love may wish for something more substantial. Your picnic menu can be as wonderfully varied as the feast's location.

A summer picnic, for example, might include chilled shrimp cocktail, a cool gazpacho, cold broiled chicken, and a fresh peach pie in addition to a loaf of crusty bread and wine chilled to just the right temperature.

A winter picnic could include a hearty vegetable soup transported to the picnic site in a Thermos bottle, and T-bone steaks grilled on a hibachi. Potatoes can be baked ahead of time, wrapped in foil to preserve their warmth (they make terrific hand-warmers!), and reheated on the grill just before serving. Return to your home for a soak in the hot tub or a warm, relaxing bubble bath for two. Top off the evening with a flaming dessert such as Bananas Foster or Cherries Jubilee.

To provide a musical background, you may wish to bring along a portable tape player and play some of your favorite cassettes. If one of you plays the guitar, you may serenade your partner. Or simply relax and listen to nature's chorus of insects and birds.

Take time now to review the past year and your achievements as a couple. Make plans for the following year. Present each other with a small gift, appropriately made out of paper. Renew your promises to each other, and seal your pledges with a kiss.

Videotape Viewing

Many couples have chosen to have their wedding ceremony recorded not only by a still photographer, but a videographer as well. Your first anniversary is the perfect occasion for reliving the tender, exciting moments of your wedding day.

Begin this just-the-two-of-us celebration by preparing dinner — together. Choose a food you both enjoy. If it's Chinese stir-fry, one can chop the vegetables while the other cooks the meat.

Or build a pizza from scratch. If you prefer more traditional, meat-and-potatoes fare, one can baste the roast while the other tosses the salad. Make your time in the kitchen more enjoyable by having all the ingredients on hand before you start.

Serve dinner on your wedding china. For a centerpiece, use flowers like the ones which graced the altar at the church or synagogue during your wedding. Flank the bouquet with a pair of tall white candles.

If you happened to save the candles from your wedding, melt them into one large candle to burn on your anniversary. Candle molds and wicks are easily obtained at hobby and craft stores. After you've molded the candle, surround it with a ring of flowers like the ones you carried in your bouquet. The florist who supplied your wedding flowers will be happy to assist you. Many couples light a "unity" candle at their wedding. Using two smaller candles, light your anniversary candle in much the same manner.

After you've lit the candle, begin your intimate dinner for two.

If you saved the top from your wedding cake, take it from the freezer and defrost it well in advance of your meal. Slice it and share it as you did at your wedding reception.

After dinner, wash the dishes together. Or, if you're feeling romantic, the dishes can wait while you dance to a favorite song on your stereo or compact disk player.

Later, turn the lights down low, pop a batch of popcorn, and switch on your VCR. Then snuggle up together as you relive your wedding ceremony — via your wedding video.

Paper Chase

If ever you've been accused of leading someone on, this is it! Lead your one-year spouse on a merry goose chase that begins with a set of clues and leads directly to you!

Write each clue on a separate piece of paper. Scent the paper with your favorite perfume (do it before you write on it, so the ink won't run). Add lipstick kisses to heighten anticipation.

The first clue might be slipped into your husband's lunch or briefcase: "Find a blanket in the closet at home." Pin the next clue to the blanket. Then direct your lover to a certain delicatessen for bread and cheese. Leave another clue at the deli to pick up wine at a certain liquor store. Another clue would send him to a florist for a long-stemmed red rose.

Keep giving clues (not too many — he'll tire of the pursuit!) until he reaches the romantic destination you have in mind. It's a good idea to set a time limit for each clue to keep the game moving. Be realistic, however. Driving across town during rush hour will take longer than five minutes.

When your spouse reaches the end of the trail, he'll find you waiting — and ready to celebrate!

Attendants' Candlelight Dinner _____

Your first anniversary is an occasion for renewing your commitment to each other. It can also be an occasion to renew your commitment to your friends, especially your honor attendants.

Whether you invite your entire wedding party or just your maid of honor and best man, be sure to include their spouses or "significant others."

Using a calligraphy pen and colored ink, write the invitations on parchment paper. (Both pens and paper are available at hobby, art supply, or stationery stores. If you don't know how to use a calligraphy pen, these stores also carry easy-to-follow instruction books.) You may wish the invitation to read like this:

> You are hereby invited
> to celebrate the
> First (Paper) Anniversary
> of the marriage of
> Tammy and Drew
> date
> time
> location

Add a few flourishes with the pen to create an attractive border, or draw a flower in the corner (it doesn't have to be perfect). When the ink has dried, roll the paper carefully and insert it into a small cardboard mailing tube (available at packaging supply stores). Address and stamp the tube, and mail it.

Decorations should be in keeping with the paper anniversary theme. Hang paper streamers from the ceiling. Make them radiate from a point directly above the center of your dining table, or have them run from a Maypole which stands in the middle of your table to a small votive candle at each place setting. You may opt for bright colors, or go with colors reminiscent of your wedding. Use your wedding china and crystal, or carry the paper theme to its extreme with paper plates, napkins, and cups.

For a centerpiece, use paper flowers. If you remember the instructions from your grade school art class, you can make paper roses from pastel tissue paper. Or use some iridescent ribbon (available from craft stores) for a new look. Instructions on how to make paper flowers can also be found at craft stores. If you're pressed for time, craft stores and some nurseries also have ready-made flowers you can purchase.

Write the names of your guests on paper horns or blow-outs and use them as place cards.

To get the party going, have guests make cone-shaped party hats out of fluorescent tagboard. Supply scissors and tape, and be prepared for some wild creations.

For dinner, julienne carrots, green onions, and celery. Layer the vegetables on top of fresh fillets of fish. Place the fish and vegetables carefully onto a square of rice paper, drizzle melted butter over the top, and sprinkle with dill weed. Fold the paper around the fish like an envelope, and place the envelopes on a baking sheet. Bake until the fish is tender and flaky. Serve with a tossed salad, warm crescent rolls, and your favorite white wine. Or, if you prefer, properly chilled champagne. For dessert, serve hot coffee accompanied by Greek baklava, with its paper-thin layers of phyllo dough and gooey honey-nut filling.

After dinner, your guests may present you with simple, inexpensive gifts appropriate to the occasion. The best man may once again offer a toast to the bride and groom, wishing them many more anniversaries to come!

Although paper is the traditional symbol for the first anniversary, in more recent times, clocks have been deemed an appropriate substitute.

A Timely Celebration _____

This "timely" celebration may be given for the anniversary couple by their attendants, or by a family member.

It begins with a simple invitation. Fold a piece of stiff white paper in half, or use a postcard. On the front, draw a clock face, or cut a picture of a clock from a magazine or catalog. Glue the clock onto the card. Underneath it, write, "It's time to celebrate!" On the inside (or on the reverse), write, "John and Linda have been married for one year. Come and have a good 'time' with them." Give the date, location, and time of the party. If gifts are to be given, remind guests that "clocks" *is* the first anniversary theme, and that only inexpensive, "fun" gifts are allowed.

If you have the time, attend neighborhood garage sales and pick up old clocks of every description. If the alarm clocks are operational, wind them and set their alarms for a certain hour — dinner, perhaps. Or, deck the halls with drawings and photos of clocks.

Divide guests into two teams. Have the two teams play Pictionary™ or Scattergories™, using an egg timer to regulate the amount of time each team has to complete its turn.

When the alarm clocks sound, call time out for a light meal consisting of a salad and sandwich bar with all the fixings. Finish the meal with coffee and a scaled-down version of the couple's wedding cake. Allow guests to help themselves to fancy mixed nuts and delicate mints.

After the meal, it's time for the anniversary pair to open their gifts, all of which are accompanied by clever little notes. For example, a small digital clock that adheres to the dashboard of a car might come with a note that says, "For all the time you're stuck in traffic." An egg timer could be billed as an "Argument Timer — when the sand reaches the bottom, it's time to kiss and make up." The sillier these "timely" inventions, the better.

Save the best laugh for last, however. That's when you box up all your garage-sale clocks and give them to the couple to take home!

Gift Suggestions

Traditional (Paper)

> stationery printed with the couple's initials
>
> post cards and stamps
>
> calendars (wall, desk or pocket-type)
>
> newspaper or magazine subscriptions
>
> paper fans
>
> paper-covered boxes
>
> monogrammed paper cocktail napkins

monogrammed paper cocktail napkins

jigsaw puzzles

paper-related items such as paperweights or paper clips

tickets to a play, concert, or sporting event

assorted gift wrapping papers and colorful ribbons

Origami instructions and paper

Modern (Clocks)

antique clock, digital clock or clock-radio

wall clock

mantle clock

grandfather clock

kitchen timer

alarm clock

egg timer

disposable wristwatch

clock/thermometer/barometer

sundial outdoor clock

Gifts to Each Other

books (poetry, or books that reflect your spouse's special interests)

art prints

sheet music (for piano, guitar, special instruments you play, or music for duets you can play together)

paper flowers

paper jewelry

papier mâché figurines

road map to a romantic hideaway

Anniversaries
Two to Five

T he second through fifth years of marriage are years of
growth. You adjust to one another's habits, you form a
closer bond between you. Small wonder that the anniversary
symbols for these years include so many growing things!

Second Anniversary —

Cotton

Cotton, soft and fluffy, is the symbol for the second anniversary. Perhaps it represents the coziness of a two-year marriage. Couples who are celebrating their second year of marriage may include others in the celebration.

Cotton Bowl Anniversary _____

If your anniversary occurs in autumn, this anniversary party will be a natural. However, you don't need falling leaves and bright-orange pumpkins to hold this football tournament! An anniversary "cotton bowl" can be held at any time of year—even in snow!

Invite your friends to a Saturday afternoon football game at a park or beach near your home. To make the invitation, fold pieces of brown construction paper in half. Draw a football shape on the folded paper, making sure one side of the football is on the fold. Cut the football so that when the invitation is opened, it looks like two footballs joined at the side. Glue a cotton ball to the outside of one of the footballs and draw a stem and leaves beneath it. Under the cotton "plant," write, "Come to the Cotton Bowl." Inside, write, "Help us kick off our third year of marriage!" List your names, and the date, time, and location of the "tournament."

When the gang arrives at the park, divide them into teams. Supply each team member with a cotton T-shirt in your wedding colors. The shirts could bear the message, "Tom and Jean's Second Anniversary Cotton Bowl." Establish boundaries for the gridiron, then play a friendly game of touch football.

At "halftime," serve a "tailgate" picnic from the back of your car. Haul out a portable grill and prepare hamburgers and bratwurst. Open up an ice-filled cooler to reveal German potato salad and cole slaw. Open another and allow your guests to help themselves to beer, wine, or soft drinks (check to make sure alcoholic beverages are allowed in your local park!). For dessert, serve a sheet cake decorated with a miniature football field and the words, "Touchdown! Second Anniversary!"

If you're picnicking in a picnic shelter or at a nearby table, spread a brightly-colored cloth across the main buffet table. Stack contrasting paper plates and utensils at one end. For an unusual centerpiece, purchase a used child's football helmet from the Goodwill, Salvation Army, or a sporting goods store that deals in used equipment. Spray paint the helmet in one of your wedding colors. Turn the helmet upside down, and write your names on the sides. Set the upside down helmet on the table. Put a piece of florist's foam inside the inverted helmet. Glue or tape cotton balls to the ends of fine-gauge florist's wire. Wrap the stems with green floral tape and add some fabric or plastic leaves to make cotton "bolls." Insert the bolls into the foam. Add real or silk flowers to complete the centerpiece.

After the picnic, you may wish to resume your football game, or your guests may choose to present you with inexpensive gifts made from cotton. And, if someone asks you what your "game plan" is for the coming year, tell them it includes celebrating your third anniversary!

Harlem Cotton Club Anniversary Party _____

Recapture some of the forbidden romance of Harlem's Cotton Club at the beginning of the Jazz Age.

Turn your recreation room, basement, or apartment-complex party room into a nightclub. All it takes is some low lighting and a few elegant touches.

Start with a white tablecloth and napkins, and candles on the buffet table. Scatter mirror chips across the table. Dim the lights, or use pink or yellow bulbs. Drape a few boas on the backs of chairs. If the floor is tile or vinyl, sprinkle salt on the floor to simulate an old nightclub dance floor. (You can also use sawdust or cornstarch.) Set out replicas of old Coca-Cola™ coasters and ashtrays for guests to use.

Put a gambling table in one corner and set up casino games such as roulette or twenty-one. (Casino games can be rented. Look in the Yellow Pages under "Games and Game Supplies.") If gambling is not your style, play a jazz version of Trivial Pursuit™.

Invite your friends to attend by sending out elegant black-and-white invitations featuring tuxedos or piano keys (available at party supply stores). Or write your own:

Come to the Cotton Club
For the Second (Cotton) Wedding Anniversary
of James and Diane Spencer
Friday, July 2
456 Cotton Lane
Doors open at 8:00 p.m.
Nightclub attire optional.

Have jazz music playing in the background as you greet your guests in a torch singer's costume. (Your husband will look equally elegant in a rented tuxedo.) Take photos using an old Brownie camera with the big flash bulbs. Lip sync a blistering Billie Holiday love song to your husband. He may come up with a love song of his own!

Gift Suggestions

cotton gloves

cotton handkerchiefs

bandannas

T-shirts

cotton canvas shopping bag or book bag

beach towels

cotton table napkins or place mats

cotton wrist sweat bands

sport socks

Gifts to Each Other

cotton lingerie

monogrammed handkerchiefs

his and hers cotton terry cloth bathrobes

deluxe cotton sheets and pillowcases

Mexican rope hammock

cotton sweaters

collection of jazz tapes or compact disks

Third Anniversary—

Leather

Durability is one of the qualities of a good marriage. Indeed, being able to withstand the tests of time seems to strengthen relationships. Leather's ability to withstand wear and tear may have contributed to its selection as the third anniversary symbol.

American West

If the Hollywood Westerns are a reliable source of information, citizens of the Old West lived in a world of leather—leather boots, leather chaps, leather saddles. Celebrate your third anniversary with a wild-west theme.

Round up your friends with invitations printed on genuine leather. You can purchase leather pieces from hobby and craft shops, or fabric stores. A shoe-repair business is another source of leather scrap. Use an indelible fabric marker or a wood burning tool to write the party information on the leather. You may wish to outline the words with a picture of a cowboy boot. Inform your guests that this is your third wedding anniversary, and that they should wear something made of leather to the party so they will be in sync with the party theme. Include the date, place and location, and a phone number guests can call to accept or decline your invitation.

Party rooms or recreation rooms in an apartment complex are good places to hold this party. Homeowners can use their finished basement or family room as a party room. For an all-out effort, instruct the gang to meet at a local riding stable, where you've rented the stable's party facilities.

Decorate the party room with Western "artifacts." Wagon wheels, spurs, cattle skulls, old leather boots all make wonderful wall decorations. So do inexpensive cowboy hats (better yet, provide them to your guests as party favors). If you own a Navajo rug, make sure it's part of your party room decor. Use bales of straw for corner fillers or for seating.

Cover the dinner table with a checkered tablecloth, or make your own by stitching together several blue and red bandannas. Place more bandannas at each place setting for guests to use as napkins. For a centerpiece, place a tall vase inside a cowboy boot and fill it with seasonal flowers. Use blue enamel spatterware or metal pie plates to serve the "grub." Serve drinks in pint-size fruit jars.

Set the table in a way that allows guests to move through the "chow line." Or, if guests will be moving past a counter, decorate the counter to look like an old-time chuck wagon. Bend a curtain rod into a horseshoe shape. Then ruffle an old sheet around it to give the appearance of wagon canvas. Allow guests to help themselves from crockpots filled with cowboy stew or chili, hot baking powder biscuits or corn meal muffins, and baked beans flavored with crumble bits of bacon or chunks of ham. Serve a blueberry or apple cobbler for dessert.

After supper, clear the floor for dancing to contemporary country music. Make sure someone can teach guests how to dance the "Texas Two-Step." Then take a breather and hold an awards ceremony. Award inexpensive prizes to the person who wore the most leather, or the most authentic Western costume. The prizes, of course, will all be leather—key chains or cases, coasters, luggage tags, or small change purses.

After the ceremony, thank your guests for helping you celebrate your anniversary. Then partner up for more dancing!

Gift Suggestions

leather belts
slippers

camera bag
leather-bound photo album
billfold/wallet
leather scrapbook
blank book with leather spine
leather passport holder
checkbook carrier

Gifts to Each Other _____

jacket or coat
cap or hat
handbag
leather gloves
briefcase
leather jewelry case
leather stud box
leather diary
leather desk set

Fourth Anniversary—

Flowers

A single rose, a nosegay, a huge bouquet. Nothing expresses love better than flowers. How appropriate, then, that the Fourth Anniversary is the Flower Anniversary.

Floral Fantasy

Express your love for each other on your fourth wedding anniversary with all the exuberance Nature can provide. Immerse yourselves in a shower of flowers!

Plan an intimate dinner for two using flowers not only as table decorations but as important ingredients in your cooking as well. For example, begin dinner with appetizers made of stir-fried squash or pumpkin blossoms. If you don't have squash or zucchini in your garden, buy some blossoms from an Oriental vendor in your local farmer's market. Dip the blossoms in a thin fritter batter and fry lightly in butter. If you wish, serve the fried blossoms with a vegetable or Ranch dip.

Or serve cream of mushroom or cream of broccoli soup. Don't forget to float some chive blossoms on top! Their lovely lavender color will look quite elegant against the creamy soup.

You can follow any soup course with a tossed salad that features flowers amid the greens. Edible flowers you may wish to use in your salad include nasturtiums, lemon marigolds, calendulas, or peablossoms (but not sweet peas—they're poisonous!). Add sunflower seeds for extra crunch. Serve the salad with your favorite meat or fish—perhaps smoked salmon—and twice-baked potatoes.

Dessert can once again feature flowers. Try decorating purchased petit fours with sugared violets on top, or vanilla ice cream with sugared rose petals. Or decorate a cake with Johnny Jump-ups.

This elegant floral dinner should, of course, be served on your best china, accompanied by your crystal and a white cloth. A floral centerpiece is most appropriate. Theme the centerpiece to the season in which you're celebrating your anniversary. Or, if you kept your bridal bouquet, use it as your centerpiece. Another alternative is to simply gather a bouquet from your own garden. Tuck a flower into your hair, and pin a boutonniere on your husband's lapel.

Scent the air with floral potpourri. Light a pair of romantic tall white candles. Or scatter votives around the room, flanked by small, fragrant bouquets.

After dinner, you and your loved one could go out onto your deck or patio (weather permitting). Toss a blanket on the floor, and enjoy spring water in fluted champagne glasses. If you have a hot tub or spa, float fresh roses in the water and delight in their fragrance as they swirl around you.

Gift Suggestions

flower vase

cut flowers

potted flowering plants

spring flowering bulbs

amaryllis plant

seed catalog gift certificate

silk flower arrangements

pruning shears

seed catalog gift certificate

floral scented drawer liners

Gifts to Each Other

floral paperweight

rose bushes

floral fragrance

perennial flower garden book

floral patterned bed sheets

Language of Flowers book

glass dome (for displaying your bridal bouquet)

floral print poster

Fifth Anniversary—

Wood

A couple who has reached their fifth anniversary have solidified their relationship—hence, wood becomes a perfect symbol for anniversary number five.

Tree-planting Ceremony _____

Recall your wedding day and create precious new memories as well.

Begin by inviting a few close friends to attend a tree-planting ceremony in your back yard. Make the invitations by cutting out Christmas-tree shapes from folded green construction paper. Write a large numeral five on the outside. Underneath it, write, "Five Years of Growth!" Inside, write, "Help us celebrate our Fifth Wedding Anniversary! Since wood is the symbol for this anniversary, a tree-planting ceremony will be held (date, time, location)."

Dig the hole for the tree before your guests arrive (this saves time and spares your guests from watching you perspire). Drive spikes into the ground around the hole and cordon the area off with ribbon to keep guests from accidentally falling in. Tie a matching ribbon to the shovel you will use during the ceremony.

Decorate your deck or patio with paper Japanese lanterns or strings of miniature Christmas lights. A checkered tablecloth on the picnic table signals to your guests that this is an informal affair. Fill a woven wooden berry basket with fresh flowers for the centerpiece. Keep the blossoms upright and perky by arranging them in florist's foam soaked in water.

Have guests arrive in late afternoon. Greet them with cool drinks. Or offer them fruit punch served with pieces of fruit on a wooden skewer. Allow guests to help themselves to crackers and assorted cheeses on decorated toothpicks while you light the grill and cook shish kebabs made of lamb, green peppers, and onions brushed with olive oil, garlic, and herbs. Serve the kebabs to your guests on paper plates nestled within bamboo or wicker plate holders. Add a hearty red wine, more fresh fruit and cheese, and baskets of warm, crusty bread.

Later, as dusk falls, switch on the party lights. Then gather all your guests to help you plant your anniversary tree.

You may wish to plant an oak, for its solidity, or a pine that symbolizes the "evergreen" character of your love for each other. Or you may prefer a tree that adds seasonal color to the landscape such as a flaming red maple (flaming passion) or a flowering crab ("Love springs eternal"). Whatever type of tree you choose, be sure to follow the planting directions provided by your local tree nursery.

One of you should make a speech: "We have been married for five years now. And in that time, our love for each other has grown, more than we could ever have imagined. We're planting this tree tonight as a symbol of our love—living, growing, weathering all kinds of storms, and withstanding the tests of time."

Together, the two of you should lower the tree into the hole. Ask a friend to hold the tree upright as you take turns shoveling dirt around the roots. Then water it well.

When the planting is completed, someone may propose a toast: "To Dave and Amy—may their marriage continue to grow and prosper—like this tree!"

Gift Suggestions

wooden baskets

Shaker boxes

bookends

wooden name plate

salad set

wooden trays

wine rack

fireplace kindling bundles

Gifts to Each Other _____

wooden sculptures or carvings

curio cabinet or wooden shelves

hairbrush sets

cedar-lined closet

laser-carved wooden desk sets or boxes

willow "twig" garden or porch furniture

nest of folding tables

croquet set

quilt rack

ping pong table

wicker furniture

bentwood rocker

Anniversaries
Six to Ten

B y the time you've been married six or more years, you've become settled in your relationship. You may have purchased your first home, or started a family. You're advancing in your career. Finding time for each other may not always be easy. However, there's still one day each year when your relationship should take precedence above everything else — your wedding anniversary.

Sixth Anniversary —

Candy or Iron?

Candy or sugar has long been the symbol for the sixth wedding anniversary. Yet, in some areas, iron is preferred. Whichever symbol you choose will be the most appropriate for your celebration.

The Sweet Sixth

Candy is handy — especially when you use it as the basis for a sixth anniversary celebration! Invite your friends over for an old-fashioned taffy pull.

Purchase wrapped taffy at a local candy store. Glue the candies to a folded 6" x 9" white card. On the inside, write, "Joe and Arlene are sweethearts still! Help us celebrate their sixth wedding anniversary with an old-fashioned taffy pull!" Add the date, time, and location. Ask guests to bring inexpensive candy-making supplies as gifts.

Decorate your kitchen with red and white streamers. Wrap the handles of large wooden spoons with red and white plastic tape to resemble candy canes. Twist pieces of iridescent ribbon into butterfly shapes and tape them to the walls.

As guests arrive, hand them each an apron. Divide them into two teams — men vs. women, or couples vs. couples. Assign each team to a pot of boiling sugar syrup. One person can stir while another reads the candy thermometer. Another can butter a cookie sheet, platter, or marble slab. Still another can hand ingredients, such as food coloring or flavorings, to the candy cook. When the thermometer says the taffy mixture has reached the soft ball stage, take the pot from the stove and pour its contents onto the platter, cookie sheet, or slab. Have team members butter their hands. As the taffy begins to cool, teams should pull and stretch it, doubling the mixture back upon itself until it becomes light-colored. As it becomes lighter, each team pulls the taffy into one-inch ropes and lays them out on pieces of waxed paper to harden. Cut the ropes into bite-sized pieces and wrap them. Guests may take the candy home with them as favors.

After the taffy pull has ended, present the anniversary couple with a custom-made greeting card featuring an assortment of candies. Glue the candies (in their wrappers) to a piece of poster board. Printing carefully, use the candies to fill in the following message:

> Dear Joe and Arlene,
>
> A *Starburst* in the sky the day you two were married and exchanged *Kisses* at the altar. A *Symphony* filled the air (along with *Snickers* and a few *Chuckles*).
>
> Since then, you've had some *Carefree* times with your *Bit O'Honey*. You've also learned what *LifeSavers Paydays* can be.
>
> No one can accuse you of being *Airheads* or *Nerds,* but you can be little *Rascals.*
>
> We wish you the continued *Bounty* of a good marriage, and *Mounds* of *Good and Plenty* in the years ahead.

Each couple should sign the card at the bottom, then present their sixth anniversary gifts to the celebrants.

Back in the privacy of their own home, the couple may want to embark on a candy kiss hunt. Hide Hershey's kisses throughout the house. For every kiss found, the couple exchanges a special heart-felt kiss. If the candy is hidden cleverly, the kissing could go on for days!

With everyone watching their diet these days, you may find it easier to substitute iron for candy.

The Archaeological Dig _____

Iron artifacts have been found in archaeological digs throughout the world. From cooking pots to hair ornaments, many an iron implement has become a museum piece. Fete the anniversary couple by inviting them on a "dig."

Invite the couple and other guests with a map showing the location of nearby park. The map should bear the legend, "Steve and

Kathy's Sixth Anniversary Archaeological "Dig." Give the date and time, and note that refreshments will be served. On the invitations to other guests, note that this is the couple's "Iron" anniversary, and ask them to bring inexpensive gifts that go along with that theme.

As guests arrive, pair them up and send them on a hunt for the "Iron Medallion." Give each pair a different clue to begin the hunt. They will find a new clue at each site. The first pair to return to the starting point with the medallion wins.

To make the medallion, cut a medium-sized circle out of cardboard. Glue alphabet macaroni onto the cardboard, using letters that spell out the names of the anniversary couple, and the date. Allow the glue to dry. Then spray the medallion with silver paint. To give the medallion the appearance of iron, allow the paint to dry, then over-spray the medallion with dulling spray (available at hobby stores). Hide the medallion in a special place in the park.

Award the winning archaeologists with small garden tools to remind them of the *"dig"*. Give refrigerator magnets to the others as consolation prizes.

Offer refreshments to your guests as they straggle in. Depending on your budget, you may offer a full-blown picnic supper, or coffee and dessert.

After refreshments, congratulate the couple on their anniversary. If you wish, present them with a pair of horseshoes for "continued good luck in the years ahead."

Gift Suggestions

Candy

assortment of after-dinner candies

candy thermometer

marble slab (for cooling candy)

candy molds

candy recipe presented with required recipe supplies such as sugar, corn syrup, baking chocolate, nuts

candied fruit

Iron

wrought-iron bookends

magnets

wrought-iron plant hangers

cast-iron matchbox

cast-iron boot scraper

decorative iron doorstop

cast-iron cooking utensils, such as a frying pan, corn muffin pan or Dutch oven

Gifts to Each Other

Candy

specially-wrapped boxes of fine-quality chocolates

unique candy dishes

a special home-made "candy of the month" for the entire year

a year's supply of your spouse's favorite candy

Iron

fireplace utensils

antique iron coffee grinder

wrought-iron porch or patio furniture

iron garden sundial

decorative weathervane

wrought-iron birdcage

Seventh Anniversary —

Wool, Copper, Brass

Wool, copper, brass. Seventh-anniversary celebrants have a lot of symbols to choose from.

Reassessment Weekend _____

The seventh anniversary seems to be a landmark for many couples. It's a good year to take stock of where you've been and where you're going!

Make reservations for a weekend at your favorite vacation spot, or try out that new bed-and-breakfast place near your home. Leave the kids with Grandma and your cares at home. Your seventh anniversary comes only once, and you've earned the right to spend it together.

Take long walks. Simmer in the hotel whirlpool. Sleep late, undisturbed by Saturday-morning cartoons. Discuss your goals, ideas, and dreams for your home, your dual careers, and your family. A relaxed conversation over a slow, easy meal can help rekindle the fragile flame of love that can be so easily buffeted by job and family pressures.

Renew your commitment to each other. It doesn't have to be a grandiose gesture. Simply resolve to spend more time together, and seal your pledge with a kiss. Give each other a thoughtful little gift.

Gift Suggestions _____

Wool

crocheted afghan

woven stadium blanket

wool-lined gloves, mittens

Copper

cooking utensils

tea kettle

hammered copper vases or plates

copper bracelet

Brass

planter

miniature brass clock

waste basket

candlesticks

candy dish

brass coat hangers

Gifts to Each Other _____

Wool

wool muffler, with tickets to an ice-skating arena or show

Pendleton shirt or suit

Icelandic wool sweaters

satin-trimmed wool blanket

Copper

wind chime

punched copper ornaments

pair of carriage lanterns

Brass

picture frame with your photo in it

engraved desk set

figurine

fireplace utensils

desk clock

brass door knocker

brass telescope

Eighth Anniversary —
Bronze

Bronze is an alloy of two metals — a fusion of copper and tin. Marriage is a fusion, too, bringing two families together. Celebrate that fusion — that alliance — by inviting both sets of parents to share in your eighth anniversary.

Bronze Brunch

Chances are, after eight years of marriage, your two families have been brought together at various social occasions. Bring your parents together once more for your bronze anniversary.

Prepare a simple brunch at your home. Begin with hors d'oeuvres — crab-stuffed mushrooms, rumaki (chicken livers seasoned with soy sauce, wrapped in bacon, and broiled), French bread and brie. Don't forget the champagne. After all, this is a celebration! Follow up with a baked omelet and slices of fresh melon or strawberries. For an additional treat, serve a flavored coffee.

Use bronze as the key for decorating your table. Start with a plain tablecloth in a bronze or rust color. Add napkins in a contrasting color, such as yellow. For a centerpiece, place a block of florist's foam in a brass bowl. Using silk flowers, dried eucalyptus, and dried baby's breath, create a "bronze" bouquet. Or place several bright yellow daffodils in a tall glass vase. Green ferns and tall white candles can be added to complete the look.

Or start with a basic white or ecru tablecloth. Run an iridescent bronze ribbon (available from florists or craft stores) around and about the table. Make quick and easy napkin rings by tying the ribbon around rolled-up napkins. Place a blue hydrangea in a clay pot tied with the same ribbon on the table as your centerpiece.

Purchase two small bronze stand-up picture frames. Type the dinner menu in script type or write it in calligraphy. Bill the menu as "Jean and Jon's Eighth Anniversary Brunch." Insert the menus into the frames, and stand one on each end of the table.

Your parents will probably express amazement that eight years have passed "already." Ask them to help you dedicate a monument to the passage of time — a new bronze sundial for your garden. Place the sundial so that its style casts no shadow at high noon. Perhaps they will present you with a little bronze plaque commemorating the event. But don't be too surprised if they present you with another bronze object — your baby shoes!

Gift Suggestions

wind chimes

bud vase

bowls

miniature picture frames

bronze bar accessories

personalized bronze-colored balloons

bronze bookmark

Gifts to Each Other _____

bronze sculpture

sundial

umbrella stand

Ninth Anniversary —

Pottery or Willow

The everyday simplicity of pottery speaks volumes when it's used as the Ninth Anniversary symbol. Like a marital relationship, it's fragile, and must be protected. Yet, it's tough enough to be part of daily life. Willow, too, is a durable material.

Pottery Picnic _____

If the two of you haven't picnicked alone together in quite some time, your ninth anniversary provides the perfect excuse.

Be romantic. Travel to your picnic site by canoe or rowboat. Select a quiet spot where you can spread a blanket or tablecloth. Bring along a couple of pillows for truly decadent lounging. Gather wildflowers along the way (Make sure the ones you pick aren't protected species!), and place them in a stoneware pitcher for your centerpiece.

If you like, wear romantic clothes — a flowing dress decorated with bits of lace, a large, floppy hat. Or weave a garland of flowers for your hair. Place a flower in your husband's buttonhole or hat band. Give your wife a wrist corsage.

Since you have a boat to transport your belongings, you can dine in elegance on stoneware dishes. Carry the dishes — and your meal — to the picnic site in large willow baskets. Feast on bread and cheese and thick slices of smoked turkey and Virginia ham. Share a flask of wine. Feed each other grapes, or slices of apple.

At the right moment, present each other with your anniversary gifts. They needn't be large, or expensive. But they should convey your love, and thoughtfulness.

Gift Suggestions

Pottery

vases

coffee mugs

whimsical candy dishes

tea sets

table lamps

serving dish

fluted quiche dish

Willow

willow baskets with a loaf of homemade bread

willow napkin rings and napkins

Gifts to Each Other

Pottery

pottery figurines (Hummel, Precious Moments™)

collector's beer steins

Toby mugs
collectible miniature houses
Willow
Wicker porch furniture
willow "twig" furniture
year-old weeping willow tree

Tenth Anniversary —

TIN

A decade of married life! Didn't the first ten years fly by fast? As you begin the next ten years, take time to celebrate!

Tent Party

Round up the gang and rent a big, striped tent! It's time to party!

Using a felt-tipped pen, invite your friends to a backyard barbecue, writing the invitation on thin squares of tin. Give them the date, time, and party location. If you like, mention the fact that it's your tenth anniversary.

Go to an agency that rents party supplies and rent a large tent with open sides, and portable barbecue pit. Hang tin wind chimes from the trees, and tie helium-filled balloons to the backs of folding chairs. If you have the money, hire a live band. (Be sure to check with your local police department about noise ordinances in your community. You may need a permit.) Play a selection of romantic country music hits. Songs you may want to include are "Deeper Than the Holler," by Randy Travis, "Lost in the Feeling," by Conway Twitty, "Crazy," by Patsy Cline, "May I Have This Dance?" by Anne Murray, and "I'd Love You All Over Again," by Allan Jackson — a real tenth anniversary song!

Set up a buffet table under the tent. Cover the table with a checkered tablecloth. Have plenty of matching cloth napkins on hand for your guests (barbecue sauce can be sticky). For a centerpiece, fill an old tin coffeepot with daisies and black-eyed Susans. In keeping with your "tin" theme, use aluminum or tin pie plates as dinnerware.

Offer your guests their choice of beverages as they arrive — in tin cups, of course! (You should be able to find them at camping-supply stores.) Then stoke up the coals and begin to slow-cook racks of spare ribs. Add a big pot of baked beans, potato salad, and trays of fresh tomatoes, cucumbers, carrots and celery, and you've got the makings of an anniversary feast! For dessert, serve batches of gooey homemade brownies and ice cream with a selection of toppings.

For party favors, go to a toy store and purchase several tin whistles. Place the whistles inside empty tin cans decorated and painted with flowers and the words, "Joyce and Warren, Tenth Wedding Anniversary," and the date. (Use paint markers to do the job quickly and easily. You can find them at hobby shops.)

Even though you may have requested only your guests' "presence," don't be surprised to receive a few simple gifts or congratulatory cards. Before the festivities end, find a moment to thank your guests for attending the party, and tell them you'd like to see them all at your *twentieth* anniversary party!

Gift Suggestions _____

   painted tin boxes

   tin toys

   punched tin tree ornaments

   Mexican wall sconces

Gifts to Each Other _____

   candlesticks

   tin snips or cutters

   Shaker pie safe with punched tin panels

   antique tin bank

   painted tin serving tray

Anniversaries
Eleven to Fifteen

Anniversaries tend to take a lesser role in a couple's life together after the first ten years. Pressures of family life make more demands on both partners. It's hard, sometimes, to take time for each other — especially when you're hard pressed finding time for yourself! That's what makes these next five anniversaries so important!

Eleventh Anniversary —

Steel

Strong, yet malleable. Those are the qualities displayed by steel. No other metal could so aptly symbolize the strength of your marriage!

Jamaican Steel Drum Party _____

Give an eleventh anniversary a Caribbean feeling by holding a Jamaican beachcomber's party.

Invite guests to attend with the following invitation: Fold a plain white card in half. On the outside, write, "What do fishing lures, a steel drum band, and Jane and Jim have in common?" Inside, write,

> a. Fishing lures are made of steel.
> b. Steel drums are made of steel.
> c. It's Jane and Jim's "Steel" Wedding Anniversary!
> Join in the fun at a Jamaican beach party!

Give the place, date, and time, and tell guests to come in their "finest" beachcomber wear.

Hold the party at a nearby beach if weather permits. Or, book a party by a hotel pool. Decorate the party area with palm trees — real or paper ones you rent or buy from a party-supply company. Scatter patio tables and chairs throughout the party area. For centerpieces, split some coconuts in half crosswise, drain the liquid, and place a votive candle in the center. Surround the coconut with bright hibiscus blossoms. If the party is held outdoors, light the perimeter of the party area with tiki torches.

As guests arrive, give them floppy straw hats decorated with fishing lures (large spoon-types will work best) painted with the names of the anniversary pair and the date. Offer them the Caribbean beverage of their choice—tall piña coladas, Jamaican rum and colas, or malta, a sarsaparilla-type root beer.

Serve a Caribbean-inspired meal, beginning with shrimp cocktail, followed by roti — curried chicken wrapped in a flour tortilla. Serve the roti with a salad of rice, shredded coconut, and diced papaya. Offer large platters of fresh pineapple and fancy pastries for dessert. Keep the food coming until all have eaten their fill.

Lend a background beat with tape recordings of Reggae music, old Harry Belafonte island ballads, or a steel drum band. Or hire a band, if you have the resources. Stage a limbo contest, and award small prizes made of steel — fishing lures, pocket knives, tiny pairs of scissors, manicure sets, or sewing needles — to the best dancers.

At the close of the evening, the anniversary couple should thank their guests for coming to the party. Tell the couple you'd like to see them stay married for another eleven years. But watch out — if the party is held poolside, you may end up in the water!

Gift Suggestions

stainless steel teapot

two-drawer filing cabinet for the couple's home office

bread tray

stainless steel colander

toaster

corkscrew

set of four fruit knives

Gifts to Each Other

carving set

hand tools

stainless steel watch

stainless steel flatware

sportsman's knives (buck knife, fillet knife, pocket knife)

pair of fine stainless steel sewing or embroidery scissors

harmonica

wine cooler

Twelfth Anniversary —

Silk or Linen

As couples grow in their relationships, they form a deeper appreciation for each other — and for the finer things in life. Small wonder, then, that silk or linen — two of the finest fabrics in the world — are the chosen symbols for the twelfth anniversary.

Arabian Nights Silken Fantasy _____

Have you dreamed of sleeping in a castle? Or bathing in a heart-shaped tub heaped with bubbles? Or in a cave with leopard-skin coverings on the bed? Across the country, a new kind of luxury hotel has emerged, with guest rooms decorated to cater to almost every fantasy. If such a hotel is out of your budget (or you can't find one in your area), create your own Arabian Nights fantasy.

Begin with pillows. Lots of pillows. Scatter them, pile them — all around your living room floor. Place two large ones on the floor next to your coffee table.

Lower the lighting. Better yet, light the room with candles. Sprinkle dozens of votive candles on tables, on shelves, in little niches. If you have a fireplace, light a fire, and move the coffee table in front of the hearth.

Set a table for two at the coffee table, using your best linen place mats and napkins. Place a simple bowl of dried fruits — apricots, dates, figs — in the center. Or substitute a bowl of fresh fruits, if you prefer.

Play some romantic music softly in the background. If you're really in an Arabian Nights mood, play Rimsky-Korsakov's "Scheherazade."

Begin your just-the-two-of-you dinner with bowls of steaming, home-made chicken soup, followed by roast leg of lamb on a bed of saffron rice. Serve wine, if you like. End the meal with wedges of fresh melon, sticky-sweet baklava, and strong, black coffee.

Feed each other dried fruits as you read *Tales of the Arabian Nights*. Or lose yourself in the ambiance of this intimate occasion. Give each other intimate gifts.

Gift Suggestions

Silk

scarves

sweaters

long underwear (for skiers and outdoor enthusiasts)

Linen

handkerchiefs

shirt

dish towels

hand towels

Gifts to Each Other

Silk

negligee/peignoir set

pajamas

jacket

evening bag

blouse

briefs

Linen

linen bedspread

jacket

throw pillows

shirt

dress

Thirteenth Anniversary —

Lace

Lace is the symbol for the thirteenth anniversary. Perhaps its delicate patterns suggest the delicate care needed to maintain a marital relationship.

Victorian Lace Breakfast in Bed _____

Deck yourself — and your bedroom — in yards of lace-trimmed fabrics for a romantic, Victorian atmosphere. Then serve breakfast in bed!

Prepare your favorite breakfast — an elegant quiche, perhaps, or the tried and true bacon, eggs, and coffee. Or have a very *un*-Victorian breakfast of champagne, chocolates, and strawberries.

Place a lacy paper doily on each breakfast tray, then set the trays with your best china and silver. Place a small bud vase on each tray, and place a single rose in each vase. Arrange the food on the plates, cover them, and place the trays on a tea cart. Wheel the cart into the bedroom. After you set the trays on the bed, let in the morning light.

If you're a devotee of flannel nightgowns or pajamas with feet, toss them aside today. Greet your beloved wearing a lacy confection that would make Queen Victoria blush — a long, flowing peignoir, perhaps, or a racy teddy.

Wish each other a happy anniversary, and say hello to another year of marriage

Wilkie Collins Moonstone Mystery Party _____

Moonstone is a form of feldspar treasured by jewelry makers for its pearly translucence. It's also a less well-known symbol for the thirteenth wedding anniversary. The Moonstone was also a large yellow diamond that figured prominently in Wilkie Collins' *The Moonstone,* published in 1868. Why not celebrate your thirteenth anniversary with a little mystery of your own?

In some cities, there are dinner theatres or hotels that offer "Murder Mystery" evenings, where guests are invited to play sleuth and solve a crime. Some bed-and-breakfast establishments offer entire weekend packages built around that type of theme. If so, make reservations for you and your spouse to attend. It's a great way to get some time to yourselves and to meet new people.

If such entertainment options are not available in your area, stage a "whodunit" party in your home. Invite your personal attendants and their spouses, or other close friends for an informal evening of snacks and party games such as Clue™ or How to Host a Murder™.

Issue the invitations on plain white postcards. On one side, draw a huge question mark. On the reverse, write, "Mysterious Moonstone Anniversary Party," and give the date, place, and time. If you'd like, go to the Salvation Army or Goodwill and assemble some inexpensive "costumes" for your guests to wear as they act out their parts.

Be prepared for some laughs as they attempt to shift the blame elsewhere!

Gift Suggestions

Lace
lace handkerchief

lace collar

Quaker lace tablecloth

lace-edged towels

lace-covered throw pillows

Moonstone (feldspar)
pendant

tietack

necklace

Gifts to Each Other _____

Lace

lace teddy

lace peignoir set

lace curtains for your bedroom

Moonstone (feldspar)

cuff links

tie tack

drop earrings

ring

Fourteenth Anniversary —

Opal

Ivory is the traditional motif for the fourteenth wedding anniversary. Today, much of the ivory on the world market has been obtained by poachers who slaughter African elephants solely for their tusks. To preserve an endangered species and discourage poachers, we suggest you substitute opal for ivory.

Australian Outback Barbecue _____

Opal is a pale stone with fiery lights in its core. The most beautiful opals come from Australia, where mines produce not only white opals, but precious black ones as well.

Australians love to barbecue, so why not celebrate your fourteenth wedding anniversary with an Aussie-style barbecue?

Invite your friends and relatives with an informal telephone call. Explain that it's your "opal" anniversary and you'd like to celebrate with an Australian barbecue. Blue jeans and casual shirts are required; floppy "bush" hats are optional.

Contact a local travel agent or the Australian tourism bureau nearest your home and ask if they have any travel posters you can purchase for decorations. If you have a flagpole in your back yard, hoist the Australian flag for the day. If you've been to Australia, be sure to put your souvenirs on display.

If you have tablecloths with aboriginal designs on them, use them. Otherwise, use bright-colored cloths in yellow, orange, and red. Give them an aboriginal "look" by painting them with your hands dipped in white paint and pressed palm-down on the cloth.

Purchase tiny stuffed koala bears as party favors. They can usually be found in novelty shops, clinging to a string. Use them to clasp little cards bearing each guest's name.

The party menu could include grilled chicken, an Aussie favorite. Or how about steak, grilled, and topped with whole peppercorns? Be sure to have plenty of Australian beer on hand to wash it down. For a vegetable, you could serve pumpkin, baked as you would a squash, and offered up with butter, salt and pepper. Dinner can end only one way — with Pavlova, a dessert created by an Australian chef who wanted to honor the great ballerina, Anna Pavlova. It's a sinful concoction of baked meringue topped with whipped cream and slices of strawberries or kiwi fruit, or drizzled with passion fruit sauce.

For a musical backdrop, go to your local library and check out recordings of Australian aboriginal chants and perhaps a didgeridoo — a four-foot-long log or tree branch that makes weird and wonderful music. You can be sure everyone will want to join in on folk songs such as "Waltzing Matilda." Don't be surprised if they follow up with "For He's a Jolly Good Fellow" and "Let Me Call You Sweetheart!"

Gift Suggestions

    letter opener with opal inlay

    tie tacks

    stick pins

Gifts to Each Other

- opal and diamond pendant
- oval opal ring
- opal double drop earrings
- bracelet
- opal mosaic stud box
- trip to Australia

Fifteenth Anniversary —

Crystal

When you reach your fifteenth anniversary, you've come to the first of the big anniversary celebrations. And, indeed, fifteen years together is something to celebrate!

Cinderella's Crystal Ball

Perhaps you couldn't afford a big wedding reception. Or maybe you didn't want one . . . then. But now you've been married for fifteen years, and you have the resources. Why not celebrate?

Begin by booking the ballroom of a local hotel or country club. If your party will not require that much space, rent a small meeting room and have the hotel bring in a portable dance floor (expect to pay extra for it).

Then hie thee to a printer and have the following invitations made:

> Cinderella met Prince Charming
> at a crystal ball
> please join us
> in celebrating
> our Crystal Anniversary

Be sure to include the date, place and time. If this will be a "black tie" occasion, print this on the invitation, too.

Hire a three– or four-piece band or orchestra, or a disc jockey. (Make sure the music will not overpower the room.) Your guests will want to converse and catch up with each other, as well as dance. Be sure to give the band leader or disc jockey a list of any favorite songs you will want played.

Work with the hotel's catering manager to determine the amount of food you will need. Remember that a served dinner usually costs less than a buffet, and is more elegant. For the fun of it, ask the hotel to provide a wedding cake. Top the cake with crystal wedding bells, cherubs, or lovebirds. If you're really feeling extravagant, order an ice sculpture. (Have fun with this. Ask for a pair of lovebirds, a heart, or Cinderella's slipper!) Hang a mirror ball in the center of the room to cast spinning reflections during the dance.

Sometime toward the middle of the evening, your best man (if he is present), should once again propose a toast to the bride and groom — "To Gene and Barb, who've made their married life a fairy tale come true. May they continue to live happily ever after."

Let the party continue well after the clock strikes midnight. This is one ball you won't run out on!

Gift Suggestions

bouquet or bud vase

crystal figurines

crystal salad set

crystal bell

crystal vase

crystal sun catchers

crystal picture frame

paperweight

grow-your-own crystals

crystal ring holder

Gifts to Each Other

- crystal stemware
- crystal ring holder
- perfume bottles
- crystal decanter
- crystal candle holders
- crystal mini dome clock

Anniversaries
Sixteen to Twenty

T he anniversaries which follow the fifteenth and lead up to the twentieth are rather quiet affairs, perhaps because couples who have reached these marriage milestones are caught up in raising their families or preparing to send their eldest children off to college. It's easy to overlook an anniversary during times like these. But don't. Your relationship is just as important today as it was then.

Sixteenth Anniversary —

Topaz

Topaz is a gemstone that ranges in color from blue to a yellowish-brown. It's also a species of South American hummingbird. Why not celebrate your sixteenth wedding anniversary with a South American flair?

South American Sampler

South America is a continent of many peoples and languages, customs and cuisine. Unfortunately, there are few restaurants in the United States that offer authentic South American food. So invite your friends over for a leisurely anniversary dinner that gives everyone "a little taste!"

Party decorations for this dinner are easy — particularly if you've traveled below the Equator and returned with a few mementos. If not, you can achieve a South American "look" with a few simple pieces available at most any shopping center.

Use a colorful woven rug as a table runner. Group souvenirs or clay figurines in the middle of your dining table for a centerpiece that's sure to be a topic of conversation. Plaster the walls with travel posters. Set the table with simple stoneware dishes.

For party favors, give each guest a wooden cup on a stick with a ball attached to the cup with a string. A child's toy, the object is to toss the ball into the cup. If you like, write your names and "16th Anniversary" on the cup with a paint marker. The toys can be found at import shops and at upscale toy stores. They may be the only entertainment you need to provide!

Background music is as close as your local library, where you'll find authentic Andean flute music as well as songs from Argentinian gauchos.

Your local library is also where you'll find a vast array of cookbooks containing recipes for South American dishes.

Begin dinner with *Ceviche de langostinos*, shrimp in citrus sauce from Ecuador, served with hot buttered toast. Follow the shrimp with *Canja á Brasileira*, chicken-and-mint soup from Brazil. Serve a dry white wine with both. For the main course, offer an Argentine beef saute, flavored with onions, green peppers, and kidney beans, and served over rice. Accompany with a dry red wine. Dessert is easy with Brazilian-style bananas baked with butter, brown sugar, and coconut in orange and lemon juice.

After dinner, move out to the deck or patio (if the weather permits) and enjoy good friends and good conversation well into the night. Serve steaming espresso and chocolates.

Gift Suggestions

hummingbird figurines in crystal or china

hummingbird feeder

Latin music on a compact disk

Rio de Janeiro video

Gifts to Each Other

topaz clip/pendant

Marquise blue topaz ring

blue topaz, citrine, and diamond drop earrings

topaz cufflinks

topaz tie tack

men's oval topaz ring

private Latin dance lessons

Seventeenth Anniversary —

Amethyst

The word, "amethyst," comes from the Greek. The gemstone was thought to be an antidote to drunkenness. Even if your budget can't take you to sunny Greece, you and your loved one can take a Grecian Holiday.

Grecian Holiday _____

Think of azure seas, olive trees, the Parthenon, and whitewashed villages dazzling in the sun. You can capture some of the romance of Greece. You may find it in a cozy Greek restaurant in your neighborhood. Or you may cook up a little Grecian romance at home.

Set a simple table using a red tablecloth and napkins. Place a bud vase with a single white rose in the center. For a more peasant-like look, substitute a red-checkered cloth. Shove a candle inside an empty wine bottle and use it to illuminate your dinner table. Use simple white stoneware dishes for contrast.

Check out recordings of Greek folk music from your local library, and play them softly in the background. The library's cookbook section will also give you an ample supply of Greek recipes.

Begin your dinner for two with *avgolemono*, lemon-egg soup, followed by a salad of greens, black olives, and feta cheese. Be sure to provide plenty of thick, crusty bread. Next, serve lamb kebabs marinated on olive oil and garlic, or *spanakopita* (spinach pie). Complete the meal with grapes, melon, or gooey *baklava* and espresso.

Surprise your lover with a visit from a belly dancer. Or better yet, surprise him by performing a belly dance yourself. Belly dancing is an old and honored profession that has little to do with the "belly dancers" found in strip tease joints. Look under "Dancing Instruction" in the Yellow Pages to find a belly dance instructor near you.

Who knows? Perhaps your spouse will surprise you with a trip to Greece!

Gift Suggestions _____

amethyst paperweight*

amethyst window hangers

amethyst glass bud vase

amethyst linen guest towels

*(Amethyst is sometimes embedded in a ball of rock called a geode. When split, these geodes make attractive paperweights.)

Gifts to Each Other _____

amethyst heart ring

amethyst cufflinks

amethyst tennis bracelet

amethyst silk dressing gown

amethyst-colored his and hers sweaters

vacation in Greece

Eighteenth Anniversary —

Garnet

Garnet was a popular gemstone in Victorian times, often set with pearls to heighten its deep red color. Recapture some of the charm of those bygone days on your Garnet Anniversary.

Victorian Romance _____

Many fine Victorian mansions have been renovated into bed-and-breakfast establishments or restaurants. Make reservations for a romantic dinner for two at an establishment near you.

Relax in the quiet ambience of the mansion's high-ceiling rooms. Share a bottle of fine wine as you gaze out the lace-curtained windows. Or wander about the grounds and sip your wine in the fragrant shelter of a flower-filled gazebo. If a strolling violinist comes your way, ask him or her to play your favorite melodies. Enjoy the intimacy of candles on the table.

After dinner — go ahead, splurge on dessert! Order that sinful chocolate cake with raspberry sauce! After all, the berries are the color of garnets, aren't they? When your meal is finished, step out onto the verandah, where a horse and carriage awaits you and your loved one just below the steps. Take a slow, gentle ride around the city. Watch the lights as they twinkle in the darkness. Cuddle as you travel together to local landmarks.

Arrange to have the carriage return you to the inn, or drop you off at home. You can always pick up your car tomorrow!

Gift Suggestions _____

garnet red wine glasses

package of garnet red paper napkins

garnet red satin pillow cases

garnet red glass candy dish

Gifts to Each Other _____

garnet signet ring

garnet and freshwater pearl necklace

garnet earring jackets

garnet cufflinks

garnet red silk tie

garnet red camisole

weekend at a bed-and-breakfast establishment

horse-drawn carriage ride

Nineteenth Anniversary —

Aquamarine

Aquamarine is a combination of two Latin words, "aqua" and "marine," meaning "seawater." So spend your nineteenth anniversary near the sea!

Seashore Holiday _____

An ocean breeze, seagulls squawking and wheeling in the sun, a walk along the beach. No wonder so many romantic novels take place near the sea!

Travel to the ocean — or a nearby lake — for a special day together. Many lighthouses along the East and West Coasts and the Great Lakes are now part of state or national parks and are used as museums. Soak up some seafaring lore from the lighthouse guides as you climb the stairs to the beacon at the top.

All that climbing is sure to work up an appetite. Spread your beach towels on the shore beneath the lighthouse and unpack your picnic lunch.

Uncork a bottle of chilled white wine or sparkling water and serve it in tall fluted glasses. Toast your marriage, then dine on chilled crab salad nestled on a bed of fresh spinach leaves. For dessert, walk hand-in-hand to an ice-cream vendor and buy yourselves a couple of double-dip cones.

Relax. Spend a lazy afternoon tossing bread crumbs to the gulls and watching clouds drift by. Listen to the waves as they roll into shore. Pretend you're the lighthouse keepers. Try bodysurfing. Watch the wildlife that lives in the tide pools. Or collect seashells.

Watch the sun go down, then return home — slowly.

Gift Suggestions _____

aquamarine floating pool lounger

swimmer's goggles

beach towels

goldfish in an oversized brandy snifter

natural deep-sea sponge

tape recording of sea and surf side sounds

Gifts to Each Other _____

aquamarine pendant

aquamarine ring

a trip to the seashore

Caribbean cruise

blue-green enamel turtle pin

gold sand dollar belt buckle

gold conchs, sand dollars, and scallops bracelet

mementos that remind you of your day by the sea —
  photographs, paintings, carvings

Twentieth Anniversary —

China

The Twentieth Anniversary is often the first of the big public celebrations. It's a day that should be shared — after all, twenty years of marriage is a bit of a landmark!

Chinese Garden Party_____

Since china as we know it originated in China, why not celebrate your Twentieth Anniversary with a Chinese Garden Party?

Several weeks before the party, rent a camcorder from a rental business or a camera store. Tape the recollections of a few friends and family who were close to the couple and ask them about the couple's courtship days. Ask questions such as, "How did they meet?" "Did they have lover's spats?" "Was their romance hot and passionate or sweet and romantic?" "Who proposed?" "What was the wedding day like? Did it rain? Snow?" Edit the tape for viewing at the party.

Decorate your yard or party room with strings of Chinese lanterns. These may be the large paper ones, or the tiny ones that are sometimes used for Christmas decorations. Build a place of honor for the anniversary couple, using sections of pre-constructed redwood lattice to make a three-sided pagoda. Spray-paint the walls bright red. To make the pagoda's swooping roof, cut one out of cardboard, paint it black, and place it atop the walls. Place a picnic bench or piano bench inside the pagoda and top the bench with a cushion. If you haven't the time or talent to make a pagoda, rent a gazebo. You can find them in the Yellow Pages under "Party Supplies."

If yours will be a large gathering, call in a Chinese caterer to provide guests with an ample supply of egg rolls, steamed or fried rice, chicken wings, and sweet-and-sour pork.

If you will be entertaining a more intimate group, seat guests on cushions around a low table. Prepare the meal table side in a wok, giving meat and vegetables a quick stir-fry before serving the food to your guests. Be sure to include plenty of rice.

After dinner, play the videotape. Ask the couple the first question, then wait for their answer(s). Then switch on the television to show their friends' and families' answers. Go on to the next question, and the next. Be sure to record the couple's answers and reactions on tape, then give both videos to them as an anniversary present. It's one that will be replayed year after year!

Roaring Twenties Twentieth _____

The "Roaring" Twenties didn't roar very long, but their legacy of fun and frivolity lingers on. And what better theme for a twentieth anniversary?

Scatter lots of small tables around the party room to make it look like a speakeasy. Fill an old claw-foot bathtub (available at architectural salvage dealers) with ice and stock it with your guests' favorite "bathtub gin." If you don't want to buy a bathtub, check around. You may be able to rent one. Or, fill a cooler with ice and tape a cardboard cutout of an old bathtub to the front of it.

Place other carefully chosen antiques such as a "candlestick" telephone (a phone with the speaker mounted on the candlestick and the receiver hung on a hook on the stick) or a Victrola record player with a morning-glory speaker, around the room to add atmosphere. Reproductions of these pieces may be for sale. You may even find an antique dealer who would be willing to rent them to you for the party.

Invite guests to come dressed in fashions popular in the 1920s — anything from flapper dresses to knee-length bathing suits.

Visit your local library to get recordings from 1920s artists. Include opera stars as well as jazz singers. Play the recordings as background music.

As the party gets into full swing, clear the floor and stage a Charleston contest. Have the anniversary couple act as judges and award prizes to the pair who dances best. The couple can also award prizes for best costumes.

At the appropriate moment, offer a champagne toast to the bride and groom. When all the congratulations have been said, and the toast has been made, smash the glasses in the fireplace (or an out-of-the-way corner), and let the dancing continue 'til the wee hours of the morning.

Gift Suggestions

Wedgewood vases

China cake plate

music box topped with a china figurine

China basket

small china animal

set of four china dessert plates

china egg cups

Gifts to Each Other _____

complete china set collectible

snow houses

Precious Moments™ or Hummel figurines

china candlesticks

Hong Kong vacation

Anniversary
Twenty-five

T he Silver Anniversary is a big occasion in any marriage. Twenty-five years of wedded bliss calls for a big celebration!

Twenty-fifth Anniversary —

Silver

Sterling silver has a special quality, a purity, that sets it apart from other, lesser metals. A twenty-five-year marriage has certain sterling qualities of its own!

Traditional Silver Jubilee _____

A traditional silver jubilee contains many of the same elements as the wedding itself, including formal invitations, a cake and a receiving line.

Guests are issued invitations printed in silver ink, as described in Chapter 1. Invite as many of the couple's old friends as possible. The dates marking the beginning of the marriage and the present year are usually noted on the invitation.

The party location may be the couple's home, a church parlor, a fine restaurant, or an elegant hotel. If the anniversary will be held at home, offer simple refreshments such as tea sandwiches, mints, and nuts. Or have a caterer provide a more extensive meal. An elegant sit-down supper is also an option.

White flowers are the flowers of choice for this anniversary, and they should be used lavishly in the decorating scheme. Be sure to include a corsage for the "bride" and a boutonniere for the "groom."

Some people craft a "money tree" to serve as a focal point of the party decorations. They're easy to make. Simply spray paint a bare tree branch silver and stand it in a decorative pot, also painted silver. Depending on your preference, you can use rolled up bills as "twigs" or wrap silver dollars in clear plastic wrap, tie them with silver ribbons and hang them on the branches as "fruit." Add a few white velvet bows for a finishing touch.

The anniversary couple should stand and greet guests as they arrive at the party, just as they met them at the wedding reception twenty-five years before.

As before, a wedding cake will be presented to the couple for cutting. The silver anniversary cake differs from the wedding cake, however, with the addition of one special ingredient — a ring. Tradition holds that if an unmarried woman receives a piece of cake with the ring in it, she will be a bride within a year.

After the cake-cutting ceremony, toasts should be offered to the bride and groom. These could be long, drawn-out speeches, or simple wishes of good cheer. All should offer "long life, and a longer marriage" to the anniversary couple. As at the wedding reception, the couple should respond to the toasts, and thank their guests for helping them celebrate this important anniversary.

Now is a good time for the couple to hand out small thank-you scrolls tied with silver ribbon or bound with small "silver" wedding rings. (See Chapter 1 for suggestions on appropriate wording.)

Depending on the situation, a dance may be held after the toasts. The couple should have the dance floor to themselves for the first dance, just as they did at their wedding. If no dance will be held, the couple can invite guests to look on as they open their presents.

"Come as You Were 25 Years Ago" Party _____

If receiving lines and formality just don't fit the silver anniversary couple, you might want to opt for a more casual celebration.

Invite the couple's friends and family to a "Come as You Were 25 Years Ago" party. Take the couple's wedding photo to a printer and have it screened for reproduction. Use the photo as the cover for a folded invitation. The inside of the invitation might read,

> Come as you were 25 years ago
> to a Silver Wedding Anniversary party
> for Pat and Ray.
> Clothes worn 25 years ago suggested.
> Saturday, May 10, 1998
> 1169 Boxwood Lane
> Braintree, Massachusetts

Do a little research in your local library. If you're not sure where to begin, ask a librarian for help. Look for recordings that were popular 25 years ago, and play them as a musical backdrop throughout the evening (you may even find the couple's "special" song!) Your digging will probably also unearth some food fads of the period which you can use as the basis for a party menu.

Several weeks before the party, gather up old photos and slides of the anniversary pair and have them transferred to videotape. Have the video transfer service overdub Barbra Streisand's "The Way We Were" onto the tape.

During the party, ask the couple to act as judges in a clothing contest. They may award prizes for "most authentic costume," "loudest tie," "shortest (or longest) skirt," or "floppiest hat."

Be sure to take plenty of photos of the couple and their prize-winning friends. Shoot some videotape, too, to preserve some moving moments.

After the contest, hold a brief cake-cutting ceremony, then offer a champagne toast:

> To Pat and Ray
> For the way they were 25 years ago,
> For the way they are today.
> For the way they'll be 25 years from now —
> In love, forever.

Then play the videotape, and be sure to have a box of tissues handy.

Ethnic Anniversary Celebration _____

Celebrate your love — and your roots — with an Ethnic Silver Anniversary.

Haul those native dance costumes out of the attic trunk — or rent them. Hire a band that plays ethnic music. Sift through Grandma's recipe file for authentic dishes. Then gather the clan for old-fashioned fun!

If you've never celebrated your heritage before (perhaps, like many people, you're uncertain of your family's exact place of origin), preface your celebration with some research. Start searching several weeks before your party will take place. Old family Bibles and birth certificates often hold clues. Many states have historical and genealogical societies; check with your local society for assistance in tracking down your ancestry. The Church of Jesus Christ of the Latter Day Saints (Mormon) has the world's largest genealogical library in Salt Lake City, Utah. If there is a Mormon church near you, you may be able to trace your family through one of the church's branch libraries. Who knows — you may find yourself in an engrossing new hobby!

After you've found your roots, you should visit the cookbook section of your local library. You'll find cookbooks for nearly every type of cuisine, from Argentinian to Yugoslavian, with several stops in between. If the old family recipes never made it to your kitchen, the volumes on the library shelves should be able to help you fill in the culinary gaps. Experiment with several recipes before deciding on a final menu for your anniversary celebration.

The library will also yield information on clothing and costumes, customs, and music. You'll be able to track down state associations of people of like heritage such as the Ukrainian Americans, the Sons of Norway, or the Daughters of the American Revolution. Persons of Native American or African descent can find help at their nearest cultural center. These organizations can put you in contact with ethnic performing artists who will add a special excitement to your celebration. You may also find ethnic performers in the Yellow Pages under "Entertainment Agencies" or "Dance Companies." If dancers will be part of your celebration, you can consider renting a fraternal organization hall or a VFW or American Legion hall for the occasion. (Book early. Chances are, your anniversary may be celebrated on the same day as many weddings!)

Be sure to fly the colors of your homeland on your anniversary date. Look in the Yellow Pages under "Flags & Flagpoles" to find a store that sells both American and foreign flags.

Contact the regional tourism office for your country of origin. You may be able to get some travel posters to use as wall decorations.

Once you've located all the mood-setting trimmings for your party, invite your friends and family, and let the party begin! Who knows? Perhaps your children have become caught up in your heritage, and have arranged for a trip for two to the country of your ancestors!

Twenty-fifth Reaffirmation. _____

Many couples choose to publicly renew their wedding vows on their twenty-fifth anniversary. This may be done in their own home or at another location. The growing popularity of reaffirmations has led many churches and synagogues to write special ceremonies for the occasion. If you wish to have a religious ceremony, consult with the clergy at your place of worship.

Invite guests to attend a reaffirmation as you would a wedding. (See Chapter 1 for a sample of a reaffirmation invitation.)

You may want your best man and maid of honor to witness your vows. If, however, you have lost contact with them over the years, it's perfectly okay to ask your best friends or your children to do the honors.

Although a reaffirmation is a serious event, it is not as formal an occasion as a wedding. Wear your original wedding gown, if you like, or wear a new dress for the occasion. Carry a small bouquet, although a simple corsage may be enough. Or pin a flower in your hair. The "groom" should wear a boutonniere in his lapel.

If you will be holding the ceremony in your home or in a location other than a house of worship, choose a place at one end of the room at which to hold the ceremony. Ask a florist to construct a bower of white flowers and silver ribbons, or perhaps an archway of white and silver balloons and streamers. This will set the stage for the renewal of your wedding vows. (If the ceremony will be long, provide seating for your guests.)

Perhaps you'd like to write your own reaffirmation vows. You may wish to use something like this:

> Through joy and through sorrow
> You are my tomorrow.
> As I've pledged before
> So I will again
> I will love you forever;
> My love has no end.

After the ceremony, adjourn to another location — perhaps a fine restaurant — for a dinner reception.

White and silver should be the dominant decorating colors. Use a single white rose as the centerpiece for each table, and a large spray of roses for the head table. Place an *assaisonniere* — a small amount of salt and sugar, wrapped together in cloth and tied with ribbon. — at each place setting as a memento for your guests.

Hold a dance, if you like, or hire a strolling trio of violinists to play favorite melodies. At the end of the celebration, thank your guests for sharing your reaffirmation with you.

Gift Suggestions

silver candelabra

candlesticks

picture frame

sterling brush and mirror sets

fruit bowl

vases

a set of newly-minted silver dollars in a commemorative holder

silver tea or coffee service

flatware

sterling silver tray

silver pen and pencil set

silver letter opener

Gifts to Each Other

money clip

charm bracelet

monogrammed silver belt buckle

sterling silver pen knife

tie clip

sterling silver stud box

sterling silver compact

sterling silver pillbox

sterling silver flask
sterling decanter tags
initialed sterling silver key ring
bangle bracelets

Anniversaries
Thirty, Thirty-five,
Forty, Forty-five

C elebrated less frequently than earlier anniversaries, the thirtieth, thirty-fifth, fortieth, and forty-fifth anniversaries are special milestones. Attaining them is like adding jewels to a crown!

Thirtieth Anniversary —

Pearl

And then that maiden, so slight, so small,
That flawless and most gracious girl,
Arose in garb majestical,
A precious piece all set in pearl.
— Pearl, a Medieval English poem
Poet unknown

Medieval Madness

Was there ever a more romantic period than the Middle Ages, with its brave knights, fair damsels, and fire-breathing dragons? If your loved one still rides a white charger in your imagination, celebrate your thirtieth anniversary in a medieval manner.

Reserve a party room at a restaurant with Tudor decor, or make arrangements to have dinner catered in an art museum that specializes in medieval art. Order a large turkey or prime rib to be carved as guests pass through a buffet line that features trays piled high with fruit and marzipan candy.

Although your dress may not have

The falling sleeves, of ample flare,
. . . adorned with double pearly gems

worn by the maiden in the medieval poem, that shouldn't preclude you from wearing a pearly-white dress. Or a basic "little black dress" adorned only by a string of genuine pearls.

Decorate the dining room with framed rubbings of knights in armor, or hang a tapestry above the head table. (If your party is held in a museum, your decorating is already done!) To gather more ideas for medieval decorations, spend a day at the Renaissance Fair in your area (if there is one).

Hire a herald to announce your entry into the room with a

trumpet blast (a local college or university may even have herald trumpets to give your entrance authenticity!). If you can't find a trumpeter, check out a tape from your local library. You and your husband should pause to greet your guests as you progress through the room toward the head table.

A harpist or a medieval trio can provide musical accompaniment through dinner, but consider a juggler, wizard, or sword-swallower for true Middle Ages fun (look under "Entertainers" in the Yellow Pages).

At the height of the celebration, toast each other with a French *coupe de mariage*, saying, "You're still my knight in shining armor," or "You'll always be a fair maiden to me." Then pledge your love anew, and seal it with a kiss.

Gift Suggestions

binoculars inlaid with mother-of-pearl

boxes with mother-of-pearl inlay

letter opener with a mother-of-pearl handle

"Happy Thirtieth" painted enamel box

Oriental wall plaque with mother-of-pearl inlays

Gifts to Each Other

freshwater pearl necklace

mother-of-pearl cuff links

pearl earrings

black pearl ring or tie tack

copy of a medieval tapestry

pearl shirt studs

watch with mother-of-pearl dial

a trip to view the medieval castles of Europe

Thirty-fifth Anniversary —

Coral

Coral — pale, pink and from the sea — is used to make fine jewelry and other ornaments. Jade — white or green, and from Southeast Asia — is sometimes used as an alternate symbol for the thirty-fifth anniversary. Coral and jade are often paired together to make colorful necklaces and other jewelry. Together, they make a great pair. A thirty-fifth anniversary is a great occasion to celebrate other great pairs!

Great Couples

Think of all the great couples in history and folklore — Antony and Cleopatra, Napoleon and Josephine, Sleeping Beauty and Prince Charming. Then think of another great couple — your parents or grandparents, perhaps. Wouldn't it be fun to get all of these Great Couples together for a party?

Secure a hall, restaurant, or country club, and invite the anniversary couple's friends and relatives to a costume party featuring "Great Couples."

Make a unique invitation by recording a rap song on a cassette and mailing out copies of the message. If you're not comfortable doing a rap yourself, seek out a youngster between the ages of ten and sixteen. Rapping is an art form this younger generation knows well.

The rap might go like this:

> Great couples have come and gone
> But true love goes on and on.
> Like Romeo and Juliet,
> John and Mary are in love yet.
> Let's give a shout and a cheer
> Their marriage has reached its thirty-fifth year.
> So come one, and come all

To the Great Couples Costume Ball.
To be admitted, you must be
Dressed like a couple in history.
Like Cleopatra in her finest hour,
When she led Antony to her bower.
Or Minnie Mouse on her first date
Before old Mickey became her mate.
The party begins at half-past seven.
We're gonna create a bit of heaven.
So come on one, and come on all
To the American Legion's great big hall
On the tenth of June. We'll see you soon.

Decorate the hall with coral-colored streamers and balloons. Have tables and chairs scattered throughout the room for guests to sit. Place bud vases filled with single coral roses or dyed carnations on each table. Tie a narrow coral ribbon around each vase as a finishing touch.

Dinner should also follow a coral-colored theme. Include chicken a l'orange served with tender baby carrots, a fruit salad that contains cantaloupe and cake decorated, of course, with coral-colored frosting roses.

Hire a three– or four-piece orchestra to play the couple's favorite music during dinner, and to play dance numbers afterward.

If coming in costume is out of character for your parents' group, or the party is simply not large enough to require a costumed ball, you can still use the "Great Couples" theme. When couples arrive at the party, hand them a slip of paper bearing the names of a great couple. Other guests, as well as the anniversary couple, should try to guess who they are. Couples can drop discreet hints such as "We met in Casablanca (Bogart and Bacall)," or "We ruled Russia together (Nicholas and Alexandra)."

Before the anniversary couple opens their gifts, a toast should be proposed — "To all great couples throughout history, and to John and Mary, the greatest couple of them all."

Gift Suggestions _____

pieces of coral
coral figurines, carvings and knick-knacks from a souvenir shop

carved jade elephant

jade bookends

Gifts to Each Other _____

coral necklace

coral tie tack

coral earrings carved like rosebuds

coral cuff links

jade pendant earrings

jade cuff links

fine jade carving

jade-handled letter opener

Fortieth Anniversary —

Ruby

Bright red, and precious as a lover's kiss, rubies are the symbol for the Fortieth Anniversary. Make red the dominant color in this theme.

Ruby-colored Fortieth _____

As individuals, many of us dread turning forty, while others insist that "life begins at forty." When a couple arrives at the forty-year mark, however, it's the beginning of a major celebration!

Invite the couple's friends and family to attend a fortieth anniversary open house. Go to a printer who specializes in wedding invitations and order invitations printed on the outside with a big "40" in red foil ink. Using the same ink, the inside of the invitation should read:

Love begins at forty!
Help Jim and Julia celebrate their
Ruby Anniversary!
Open House
Sunday, June 14, 1998
2:00–5:00 p.m.
6970 Townline Drive
Memphis, Tennessee

Use red lavishly when decorating the party room. Begin with the cake table. Drape a rectangular table with a bright red cloth. Secure red, helium-filled balloons to the corners. (If you buy the balloons at a party-supply store, you may even find balloons that bear a "Happy 40th" message!)

Place the cake — decorated with red frosting flowers, of course! — on one end of the table. Carry the ruby theme a little further by having the baker separate the cake layers with raspberry filling. Substitute mounds of fresh raspberries (if they're in season) for the frosting flowers. Cut the cake early, and allow guests to help themselves as they come and go throughout the afternoon.

If cake is not enough, pile a tray high with little cherry tarts. They'll complement the ruby theme, and delight any grandchildren who may be in attendance. Fill out the table with pink mints.

Fill a bowl with red fruit punch and put it on the other end of the table. Be sure to have plenty of red napkins bearing the couple's names printed in silver foil on the table, too.

You'll give the cake table even more prominence when you place a large red paper heart on the wall behind it. Using a gold or silver glitter pen (available at hobby or craft stores), outline the number 40 on the heart. If you like, write the names of the bride and groom on the lobes of the heart, and the wedding date near the point.

Before the anniversary, have a new photo taken of the anniversary couple. Have it blown up to poster size. Get a special pen from the photography studio, and have guests write their congratulations and best wishes on the anniversary photo. Framed, it will make a wonderful memento of the occasion.

For background music, play romantic melodies from the 1940s. Or play original recordings on your stereo or CD player. Be sure to include "Ciribiribin," "I'm Gettin' Sentimental Over You," "Heart and Soul," and "Moonlight Serenade." Who knows? Perhaps the anniversary couple could be encouraged to do a slow fox trot across the party room floor!

Gift Suggestions

  ruby glass bowl
  ruby glass vase
  ruby-colored lamps
  ruby-colored sun catchers

Gifts to Each Other

  ruby and diamond stud earrings
  ruby cuff links
  ruby heart pendant
  ruby ring
  tiny animal pin with ruby eyes

Forty-fifth Anniversary —

Sapphire

Brilliant and blue, sapphires are like no other gem on earth. Set in a necklace, they resemble a string of islands — the Hawaiian Islands, perhaps. A forty-fifth wedding anniversary is the perfect time to recall the sapphire skies and seas of Hawaii. Do it with an authentic luau!

Hawaiian Sapphire Celebration _____

Transport your parents — and their friends — to Hawaii for an afternoon or evening. But don't worry about calling a travel agent — just cruise through the Yellow Pages until you reach a caterer who specializes in Hawaiian luaus.

A good caterer will be able to supply you with every thing you need to put on an authentic luau, from a barbecue pit to tiki torches. All you'll need to provide are the guests!

The caterer may also refer you to groups that specialize in Polynesian dance. If not, look under "Entertainment" in the Yellow Pages.

Schedule the party to begin late in the afternoon or early in the evening. Give the bride an orchid to wear in her hair. Have the anniversary couple greet their guests with flower leis. You can have real ones made by your local florist. If that option is too expensive, you can pick up some paper leis at a party supply store.

A party supply store will be the most likely place to find invitations with a Hawaiian motif, as well as paper palm trees and fake tapa cloth for photo backgrounds, and other props.

Allow the bride and groom to mingle with their guests until the feasting actually begins. Then have them lead the party to a groaning buffet table where Hawaiian delicacies await them.

The menu, of course, includes traditional luau foods such as roast pork, seaweed salad, and fresh pineapple and papaya. Poi, the starchy, gray-lavender staple of every Hawaiian luau is an optional menu item. If the caterer can provide it, have a small amount on hand for guests to try. Ask the caterer (or your local baker) to provide an anniversary cake with pineapple filling. Top it with a pair of Hawaiian dancers.

Have the real Polynesian dancers perform as guests partake of the meal. At the end of their performance, the dancers will probably call the anniversary couple to the performing area, where they'll be serenaded with love songs, including "The Hawaiian Wedding Song."

After the singing has ended, the couple should acknowledge the performers and thank their guests for coming to the party. Then you can spring the big surprise — a trip for two to Hawaii, from you and your siblings!

Gift Suggestions

quilt with a Hawaiian pineapple design in sapphire blue and white

sapphire-colored vase

sapphire-colored sun catchers

Gifts to Each Other

oval sapphire pendant

star sapphire ring

sapphire drop earrings

sapphire cuff links

sapphire-colored sweaters

trip to Hawaii

Anniversary
Fifty

T he anniversary books of yesteryear often cautioned against creating too much excitement for the golden anniversary couple, citing the pair's advanced age and delicate health. Today, couples celebrating a fiftieth wedding anniversary are likely to be quite active, many of them still taking a daily walk, swim, or jog well into their seventies and eighties.

While individual circumstances may vary, there's little reason to "protect" today's seniors — or to prevent them from having a good time. A marriage that lasts fifty years is a real treasure, pure gold. And a Golden Anniversary is definitely worth celebrating!

Fiftieth Wedding Anniversary —

Gold

More costly than silver, and resistant to tarnish, gold is the perfect symbol for a love affair that's burned brightly for fifty years.

Golden Anniversary Gala _____

Gold is the predominant color in this anniversary celebration. It appears in everything from the invitations to the party favors. The invitations should be printed by a reputable printing firm. Use gold foil ink to set the tone. Gold foil-lined envelopes add an elegant touch.

Decorate the party room with touches of gold. Place a raised platform at one end of the room. Cover the sides of the platform with gold foil paper. Set two comfortable chairs on the platform and flank them with large potted Norfolk Island pines. Decorate the trees with tiny white Christmas lights, golden cherubs, and gold bows.

Set up a round table off to one side of the party room. Drape the table with a white tablecloth, then cover the cloth with gold netting. Draw the netting up into scallops along the sides, and pin the scallops in place with gold velvet bows. Place an elaborate wedding cake in the center of the table; top it with fresh, full-blown yellow roses.

A champagne fountain is also appropriate on this special day. If the party will be held at a hotel or restaurant, ask the catering manager to help you with the arrangements. If the party will be held at the couple's home or some other location, you can locate fountains in the Yellow Pages under "Caterers," "Party Supplies," or "Rental Service Stores."

Install the fountain near the cake table, so that guests have a chance to "ooh" and "aah" over the cake as they get champagne. Be ready to replenish the fountain often since the circulating action of the fountain's pump tends to take the bubbles out of the "bubbly." If the couple would prefer not to serve alcoholic beverages, substitute sparkling apple cider.

Complete the aura of golden elegance by hiring a harpist or pianist to play golden favorites.

As guests arrive, have them sign in a golden anniversary guest book, available at stationery stores. Or cover a blank book with gold paper and ask guests to write in their own best wishes and congratulations on the pages.

Seat the anniversary couple on the platform. Provide a corsage edged with gold lace for the bride, and a carnation dusted with gold glitter for the groom. After guests have filed past, offering their congratulations, have the couple cut the cake and lead their guests to a buffet that includes "golden" foods such as saffron-tinted rice, elaborately carved pineapples, oriental chicken wings, and a pyramid of Golden Delicious apples. Offer gold foil-wrapped chocolate coins as party favors.

After the buffet, the couple may open their gifts. This gift-opening ceremony may include gifts to each other — new wedding bands. After fifty years of constant wear, the couple's original wedding bands have probably worn thin. The fiftieth anniversary is the perfect occasion to replace them. The rings could follow the original design, or the couple could choose to have new rings made — with room to add diamonds on the couple's sixtieth anniversary!

Fiftieth Family Reunion

If you're looking for an excuse to hold a family reunion, what better one than a Fiftieth Wedding Anniversary?

A "gathering of the clan" can take some time to organize, so start well in advance. (If your guest list will extend to several branches of the family, allow at least a year.)

Begin by choosing a location for the reunion. It may be the old family homestead, or you may wish to make group reservations at a hotel or resort. Whichever you choose, you'll probably want to hold the celebration on a weekend so that family members have plenty of time to become reacquainted.

Next, draw up a guest list. Decide how many brothers, sisters, cousins, aunts, uncles, nieces, nephews, children, and grandchildren you wish to include in the celebration. Start matching names and addresses. If you have trouble locating a certain relative, ask someone else in the family to assist you. Usually, there's an aunt or uncle in every family who keeps track of the entire tribe.

If your guest list is large, and you will be making more than one mailing, find a relative who owns a personal computer (if you don't have one yourself) and ask her or him to create a database that includes guests' names, addresses, and phone numbers. Use the list to print mailing labels. (You can also use it to make a family "directory" that guests can take home with them!)

Once you have your guest list in hand, you can take it to the resort's director of sales or catering manager and work out the details for your group. Be sure to let the resort know how many sleeping rooms you will need, if you will be dining in the restaurant or if you will require the use of meeting rooms for your group meals. Go over menu suggestions, and don't be afraid to ask for help in locating suppliers for flowers, music, and a wedding cake. Be sure to ask if a group discount is available.

For invitations, take the couple's wedding photo to a printer, and have it screened and printed onto postcards. Although black-and-white photos render the best reproductions, well-balanced color photos can also work. On the back of the photo/postcard, have the printer typeset and print the following information: "Coming soon! The Fiftieth Wedding Anniversary and Family Reunion of John and Jane Smith." List the dates and the location. Be sure to leave plenty of room on the postcard for addressing the invitation.

Later, as the reunion draws near, you may wish to provide family members with more information. If you have a writer in your family, enlist his or her aid in producing a reunion newsletter. You may wish to include a brief article about the anniversary couple's wedding — when and where it took place, who officiated, who the attendants were, what they wore (use the original newspaper account as a guide, if you can). Another article might talk about the couple's life together, and their children. If the couple prefers not to receive gifts, ask guests to contribute photos taken of the couple over the past fifty years for a scrapbook that will be presented to them during the reunion. If you will be holding the reunion at a resort, but will not be paying all the costs, tell guests that you have negotiated a group rate on rooms, and inform them of the costs.

Give guests a schedule of reunion events and activities. For example, you could plan a Friday evening dinner, followed by a roast of the anniversary couple. Encourage guests to recall humorous stories about the couple and their half-century of married life. Be sure to videotape all the silly songs and stories for future generations.

On Saturday, organize a picnic or informal buffet. If weather permits, and the party will be held at the family home, hold old-fashioned competitive games such as sack races or croquet. Stage a softball tournament at a nearby park, or organize a game of horseshoes in the backyard. If your reunion will be held at a resort, allow guests plenty of time to golf, swim, play tennis, ride horseback, or just sit and gab. For fun, provide guests with commemorative T-shirts silk-screened with the original wedding photograph.

In the evening, re-live the wedding ceremony as the couple renews their vows. Keep the video camera rolling as they cut the cake and feed it to each other. Then serve dinner, and follow it with an evening of dancing. When the band takes a break, line everyone up for a commemorative photo of the event.

On Sunday, let the clan gather once more for a wedding brunch. Present the anniversary pair with the photograph album. Allow plenty of time for sentimental goodbyes.

Who knows? Perhaps a Fiftieth Anniversary Family Reunion will become the basis for an annual celebration!

"Fifties" Fiftieth Anniversary

You needn't have married in the 1950s to hold a "Fifties" anniversary party — but it's a nice touch.

This is one anniversary celebration that's short on formality and long on fun. It's an excuse to rummage through closets and attics and dig out those poodle skirts, bowling shirts, and saddle shoes one more time.

This celebration requires no elaborate invitations; a phone call will do. If, however, you'd like to send a written invitation, consider this little poem:

Chuck Berry and Elvis have come and gone
But Dan and Jean go on and on.
So dig out your cashmere, and your bobby sox
For a Fifties anniversary that really rocks!
Saturday, May 30, 1998
1227 Wooddale Drive
6:30 p.m.
Fifties clothing a must!

Decorate the party room with high school or college pennants. Tack an old cheerleader's sweater to the wall. Set a small vase in the small end of a megaphone and fill it with flowers for a centerpiece. Make a banner that reads, "Dan and Jean — 50 years. Go, team, go!" Hang the banner above a buffet table filled to groaning with sloppy Joes, potato chips, and dips. Fill several washtubs with ice and Cherry Coke™.

For entertainment, rent a karaoke machine and allow guests to croon along to favorite golden oldies. Karaoke machines combine the melody and bass lines from old songs with laser technology. Guests sing to the accompaniment, and live pictures of them are thrown onto a large television screen. You can find karaoke machines in the Yellow Pages under "Disc Jockeys" or "Entertainers." Be sure to leave plenty of room for a dance floor for those who want to "Rock Around the Clock."

At an appropriate moment, crown the anniversary pair "King and Queen of the Prom." Present them with gold paper crowns (obtainable at party supply stores). Then make way for a romantic dance for the two of them, playing a slow number such as "Love Me Tender" or "I Can't Help Falling in Love With You."

Gift Suggestions

wine glasses rimmed with gold

gold-plated tea service

a set of gold coins, gift-boxed

gold-plated candlesticks

gold-plated candy dish

two-sided gold-plated picture frame, with the couple's wedding
picture on one side, and a current photo on the other

Gifts to Each Other _____

new gold wedding bands

gold locket with your loved one's photo inside

gold watches

gold earrings

gold nugget tie tack

gold money clip

gold chain

18-kt gold bracelet

gold-plated mirror and brush set

Anniversaries
Fifty-five, Sixty,
Seventy-five

M arriages that last longer than a half-century can only be symbolized by the most precious metals and jewels.

Fifty-fifth Anniversary —

Emerald

Really long-term marriages seem to be as rare as precious jewels. Perhaps that's why emeralds represent the fifty-fifth anniversary!

Emerald City Party _____

When Dorothy asked the way to the Land of Oz, she was told to "follow the Yellow Brick Road." Your guests — and the anniversary couple — will do the same at this party.

Send out invitations that promise your guests a good time:

> Gary and Dolly have reached the Emerald City.
> Follow the Yellow Brick Road
> and help them celebrate their
> Fifty-fifth Wedding Anniversary
> Saturday, June 8, 1997
> 7:00 p.m.
> 2225 Vale Crest Road
> Tallahassee, Florida
> Costumes optional

Draw your guests into the party via an actual Yellow Brick Road. Take a long roll of yellow vinyl and draw a brick pattern on it. Roll the vinyl out from the curb to your front door. If you want or need a less permanent "road," take yellow chalk and draw a brick pattern along the sidewalk to the door (a great job for the grandchildren!).

Since this is a special occasion, splurge on a theatrical backdrop depicting the entrance to the Emerald City. Talk to the set designer at a local theatre group, a university theatrical department, or a high school art teacher. Ask them to paint a small canvas which you can use as a background for photos of the couple and their friends and family. (It would make a great class project!) As a final touch, fill the room with bouquets of either silk or fresh poppies.

Although costumes are optional at this party, you'll want to provide some special accessories for the bride and groom. The bride, of course, is Dorothy. And, of course, no outfit will be complete without a pair of "ruby" shoes. Determine the bride's shoe size beforehand, then buy a pair of red canvas skimmers. Using fabric glue, cover the shoes with red sequins. As she enters the party room, have the bride exchange her shoes for the ruby slippers. Slip a full white apron over her head to complete the costume.

The groom is the Tin Man who's found his heart. Make a vest of silver lame' and sew or glue a bright red vinyl heart on the left side. If he can be persuaded, coax the groom into wearing a large silver funnel on his head (at least for a picture or two).

If guests choose to come in costume, there's sure to be a Good Witch Glenda in the crowd. Ask her to wave her wand over the anniversary couple and bestow good wishes upon them.

If weather and the season permit, treat guests to a Kansas barbecue featuring steak, corn on the cob, and cole slaw. Top it off with a Wizard of Oz wedding cake that substitutes figures of Dorothy and the Tin Man (available at toy stores) for the bride and groom.

After the cake is cut, someone (the Cowardly Lion, perhaps?) should propose a toast: "To Gary and Dolly, who, for fifty-five years, have known that 'there's no place like home.' They've always made us welcome in their home, and in their hearts. And that's why they'll always have a special place in *our* hearts. Congratulations to a very special couple."

Gift Suggestions _____

green-stemmed Rhine wine goblets

emerald-green glass vase

green glass candy dish

Gifts to Each Other _____

marquise-cut emerald ring

emerald tennis bracelet

emerald drop pendant

emerald tie tack

trip to the "Emerald Isles" (Ireland)

emerald cufflinks

Sixtieth Anniversary —

Diamond

Diamonds are the world's most prized gem; their rarity has increased their value. Despite longer life expectancies, sixty-year marriages are still somewhat rare, giving them a diamond-like quality.

Sixtieth Diamond Jubilee

Whether they're sophisticated and highly polished, or diamonds in the rough, couples who've reached the sixty-year mark deserve a celebration.

If the couple have been active members of their church or synagogue, hold the celebration in a meeting room or fellowship hall. If the couple now resides in a nursing home or retirement community, bring the celebration to them — and invite all the residents. It'll brighten everyone's day.

Several weeks before the party, mail pages of a photo album to friends and relatives of the bride and groom. Ask each recipient to decorate a page with a photo and a personal note to the happy couple. Reassemble the book and present it to the pair at the anniversary celebration. This works especially well for people who cannot attend the party.

Decorate the party room with silver garlands and white streamers. Toss plastic "diamonds" (available at craft stores) and silver mylar ribbons across a long table covered with a white cloth, and place the anniversary cake in the center. Top the cake with crystal doves or bells. Round out the party menu with mints and nuts, and offer guests their choice of coffee or punch.

Begin the party with a word from a member of the clergy. Then ask the couple to cut the cake. The couple's sons or daughters should propose a few toasts.

If the couple has the means, they may present each other with diamond jewelry. Or the husband may give his wife the diamond engagement ring he couldn't afford to buy sixty years ago, saying, "Diamonds are forever, and so's my love for you. I feel the same way about you today as I did when we were married sixty years ago. I couldn't afford this ring then, but I want you to have it now. But I want everyone to know that the real diamond in my life is you."

If the couple exchanges a little kiss, there won't be a dry eye in the house.

Gift Suggestions

crystal figurines

crystal suncatchers

gift certificate for a favorite restaurant

Gifts to Each Other

diamond drop earrings

diamond cocktail ring

diamond-and-onyx tie tack

diamond tennis bracelet

diamond pendant

diamond stick pin

Seventy-fifth Anniversary —

Platinum

Platinum is one of the strongest metals known. And going platinum is a term the recording industry uses when an album sells more than a million copies. Couples who are still going strong at their seventy-fifth wedding anniversary have set all kinds of records!

Platinum Anniversary Party _____

A couple that has traveled the same road for seventy-five years are special people. They've survived the ups and downs of marriage. They've shared the joy of new life as their children and grandchildren were born; they've experienced the sorrow of losing old friends. They've struggled to pay off bills; they've shared the pleasures of retirement. They've argued, then kissed and made up thousands of times. They really *have* stayed together "for richer, for poorer; for better, for worse; through sickness and in health!"

A couple such as this deserves respect, admiration, and special recognition. Do it with a Platinum Party.

(Couples celebrating their seventy-fifth anniversary are likely to be well into their nineties. Some couples may still be quite active. Others may be declining. When planning an anniversary for a platinum pair, be sure to take their health into consideration and scale the size of the party accordingly.)

Several weeks before the anniversary party, grab a video camera and arrange separate interviews of the couple. Ask them questions such as, "To what do you attribute the longevity of your marriage?" "What was your biggest argument about?" "What was your happiest moment?" "What makes your spouse so special?" "What special message would you give to your family about marriage?" Have the tape edited, and present it to the couple in a special videocassette holder at the anniversary celebration.

Since this is the Seventy-fifth anniversary, the number 75 should figure prominently in the decorations, the music, and the activities

Choose a pair of comfortable chairs for the anniversary couple and set them in a place of honor. Tape or tack the number 75 (in large platinum or silver paper figures) to the wall behind the chairs. Or have a computer-designed banner made at a local party supply store. It could proclaim, "75 Years of Wedded Bliss!," "Platinum — and Proud of it," "Still in Love After All These Years," or any other message suited to the anniversary couple.

The anniversary cake should also carry the special numeral. If it's a tiered cake, it can be placed on the top tier. (Bakers can special-order a top ornament for you.) Or have a large sheet cake made. Have the baker spell out the names of the bride and groom and the dates of their marriage in frosting on one side of the cake and a large "75" on the other.

Gather recordings of music that was popular the year the couple was married (this may take some library research). Play the songs as background music during the party.

A highlight of the seventy-fifth anniversary could be a fashion show featuring costumes worn "way back when." Dig around in the attic or in thrift stores for clothing worn around the time of the couple's wedding. If the bride chooses not to wear her wedding gown, perhaps it can be modeled by a granddaughter or great-granddaughter. There may be other articles of clothing from the bride's trousseau which can also be modeled by members of the family. Be sure to shoot lots of footage at the party, especially the fashion show.

This occasion also calls for the hiring of a professional still photographer. Photos should be taken of the couple with all their children, grandchildren, and great-grandchildren (and let's not leave out the *great*-great-grandchildren — there may be one or two!), as well as the couple by themselves. Don't forget to get candid pictures of the couple with special friends and at quiet moments during the day.

Have the photographer on hand for the cake-cutting and toasts, too. The oldest son or daughter should offer the toast: "To Mom and Dad. For seventy-five years, they've been a living example of true love. You're an inspiration to us all."

Keep the videotape rolling as hugs, kisses, and congratulations are bestowed upon the loving pair.

Gift Suggestions

Platinum picture frames for portraits of the couple, and photos of the couple and their extended family

Videotape of the anniversary party in a special videocassette holder

An old 45 rpm record spray-painted platinum and placed in a frame with a plaque bearing the names of the bride and groom and the dates of their marriage

Gifts to Each Other

platinum-and-turquoise ring

platinum charm bracelet

platinum bar pin

engraved platinum watch

Great Dates:
Anniversary
Celebrations
for Just the
Two of You

Y ou don't have to have a large public celebration for
every anniversary. In fact, some couples prefer to
recognize the occasion quietly. If you and your loved one fall into
that category, this chapter's for you!

Following are some romantic suggestions for anniversary
celebrations that are meant to be shared by two persons only. They
are not tied to a particular theme, and they can be used on any
anniversary, regardless of the year.

Anniversary High Tea _____

Perhaps the demands of two careers won't allow you the luxury of a long vacation. Or maybe your anniversary falls in mid-week. Slip away in the afternoon for a spot of tea!

Many fine hotels now feature high tea in the late afternoon. Often situated in the hotel lobby or in an open courtyard-like area, high tea offers a civilized way to spend an afternoon.

Write your spouse's name into your appointment book well in advance of your anniversary. When the day comes, leave the office for your "appointment."

Relax among the potted palms and soak up a little of the ambiance as you nibble tasty scones spread with jam or clotted cream. If tea is not quite your "cup," try a glass of sherry.

Forget about the office and talk about *us*. Make plans for a weekend getaway.

Many hotels feature a harpist or pianist during high tea. Ask him or her to play your favorite song as you give each other your anniversary gifts.

Linger over your tea. Order more if you'd like. If you find you're loathe to leave, move into the hotel dining room for an early dinner. Savor the appetizers. Order the most expensive entree on the menu. Splurge on dessert, then spring a final surprise. Lead your unsuspecting spouse to the bridal suite — booked weeks in advance!

Artful Afternoon _____

Is there a special photography exhibit you've been dying to see? Or a new museum acquisition? Whether your tastes include the Old Masters or the latest in wildlife or Western art, an afternoon at an art museum is the perfect treat for a pair of art-lovers.

Marvel over the intricacies of Japanese jade carvings. Study a Rembrandt in detail. Stand back from a Van Gogh and see how the light changes.

Talk about what life must have really been like in the court of Queen Isabella of Spain. Feel the soaring action of a Calder mobile, the eroticism of a Rodin nude.

When your senses have absorbed all they can, stop in the

museum shop to pick up a memento of your anniversary visit. It may be a coffee-table book on Impressionism. Or a reproduction of a Toulouse-Lautrec poster. You may even find a small copy of the sculpture you admired so much.

Continue your discussion of Georgia O'Keefe's paintings over croissants and espresso in a small bistro. Decide where your special purchase will hang in your home. And wish each other "Happy Anniversary!"

Business . . . or Pleasure?

On your fifteenth or other momentous anniversary, arrange an out-of-town business meeting for your spouse. Romance will be on the agenda, and the two of you will be the only ones in attendance. Only your sweetheart won't know that until you're all alone.

The ideal solution for a workaholic spouse who has difficulty leaving work behind, this "meeting" requires close cooperation from your spouse's co-workers to succeed.

Begin by booking a vacation at a mountainside retreat. Try to book more than a weekend. Your lover will be more likely to be duped into thinking it's a conference or convention if it lasts three or four days. Have his or her secretary make the necessary and normal travel arrangements, such as plane tickets and rental cars, and bill them to your credit cards. Make sure your plane will arrive at the destination before your spouse's does, by having the secretary make her or his reservations on a later flight.

Send your loved one off to work in the usual fashion, then travel to your retreat. When you arrive, tell the hotel staff that your husband will be joining you later. Then relax (if you can) in the room until he or she arrives. If possible, stock the room with flowers and champagne. Then greet your lover with open arms and a hearty, "Happy Anniversary!"

Only then will your spouse know what business is really at hand!

Champagne Balloon Flight

Take your romance to new heights when you and your sweetheart take a flight in a hot-air balloon.

Hot-air ballooning has become a popular sport in recent years. Your local Yellow Pages should yield the names of several area companies that offer champagne flights. Look under "Balloons — Ballooning."

A typical flight begins in the early morning or early evening hours when the weather is clear and winds are less than 10 miles per hour. You'll meet your balloon company representative at your home or at a designated place and drive to the field where the balloon will be launched. The pilot will already have checked the weather. If weather conditions are right, you'll fly. If not, your flight will be postponed until more favorable conditions are present. Chances are, you'll see other balloons in flight that day.

The pilot will be waiting for you. Ballooning is a participatory sport, and you'll be asked to help inflate the balloon envelope. You'll hold the throat open as cold air is pushed into the envelope with a large fan. After the balloon reaches a certain size, hot air burners are turned on to heat the air in the envelope and make the balloon stand upright. When the balloon is fully inflated, you take off.

Imagine soaring just above the treetops, so silently that you can hear children shouting and dogs barking as you pass overhead. Rivers and streams become silvery ribbons and houses take on a toy like quality. The pilot controls the balloon's altitude; the wind takes you where it wants to. A chase crew tracks your flight on the ground below.

After about an hour, the pilot will begin looking for a likely place to land. After you touch down and the balloon is securely anchored, a traditional champagne toast for a successful flight will be offered. You and your loved one can offer a second toast — to each other. Then the two of you help pack up the equipment, and return home.

Classic Camp-out

If you and your spouse love the great outdoors, an anniversary camp-out is as close as your nearest state or national forest.

Fortunately, camping can be as rugged or as luxurious as you choose. If roughing it means a trailer with electrical hookups, you'll find plenty of places to accommodate you. If it means packing ten miles into the wilderness and pitching a tent under the stars, you have that option, too.

Choose an area known for its scenery. If you're camping in the summer, reservations may be necessary in order to get the campsite you want. Whether it's high atop a granite ledge overlooking a lake, or near a pleasant little stream, you'll soon get the feeling that you're the only two people in the world.

Camping need not be limited to the summer months. If your anniversary occurs in winter, you can go winter camping. Many outfitters in northern states offer group winter camping expeditions. Others can supply you with the gear you'll need for an overnight stay in the snow. Dressed in several layers of clothing, you'll have no trouble staying warm as you ski or snowshoe across a frozen lake. A double sleeping bag shared with the one you love is one of the coziest ways to keep warm at night.

Use your camp as a base for romantic little walks through the woods to a scenic overlook, or to a meadow where wildflowers grow.

After a day of exploration, return to camp and cook supper over an open fire. Sip cups of steaming camp coffee (coffee grounds dumped into a boiling pot of water and allowed to settle). Share a small anniversary cake tucked carefully into one of the recesses in your pack.

Snuggle together as the stars come out. Pick out a pair of stars and name them for each other. You may see a meteor shower, or the Aurora Borealis (northern lights). Feel the expanse of the universe as you gaze far past the Milky Way. Then, as your campfire dies to glowing embers, enter your tent — and a world all your own.

Dancing in the Dark

Fred Astaire and Ginger Rogers made it look so easy, and so romantic. If swirling across a ballroom floor appeals to you, give yourselves dancing lessons!

Dancing instruction is offered at community education classes as well as at professional dance studios. If you think you'd like to enter competition some day (and many couples do!), the higher-priced studio will offer you the best — and more personalized —

instruction. If, however, your goal is to dance at your cousin's wedding without stepping on each other's toes, a few weeks in a community education class should spruce you up nicely.

You can also choose the type of dancing you'd like to learn, depending on your tastes. In addition to ballroom standards such as the waltz and the fox-trot, you can also learn old-time mazurkas, polkas, and schottisches; Latin tangos; disco; and Be-Bop. Or you may want to join a square dance club and learn the intricacies of executing a dosey-do or an allemande left. And don't forget clogging. Made popular in Texas nightclubs, clogging clubs and competitions are springing up everywhere in the U.S.

Whichever kind of dancing you prefer, it's a skill that transfers easily from the ballroom to your living room, where a slow dance in candlelight is all you need to set the proper mood for your anniversary.

Dinner Theatre Date _____

Discover the local talent and enjoy a lighthearted evening for two. Make reservations at a dinner theatre near you.

Share a bottle of wine as you look over the menu selections. If you're really feeling romantic, order chateaubriand for two. Enjoy pleasant conversation as you wait for dinner. Make plans for a weekend getaway — soon. Give each other your anniversary gifts after you've placed your order.

Move closer together and hold hands as the curtain rises on "Guys and Dolls," "No Sex, Please, We're British," "Oklahoma," "I Do! I Do!" or another popular musical. If the actors call for audience participation, join in the hissing, booing, cheering, or singing with abandon.

When the house lights come up at intermission, indulge in a calorie-laden dessert. Go on! Your anniversary comes just once a year!

The Kidnaped Bride/Groom _____

Love a good mystery? You'll have fun mystifying your spouse when you kidnap him or her for a romantic weekend in another city.

Pick up your lover at work on a Friday evening and drive straight to the airport. Don't tell where you're going. Then board a plane for New Orleans, San Francisco, maybe even the Virgin Islands, taking along only a few articles of clothing for each of you in carry-on luggage. (If the big cities are out of your budget, even a short flight to a neighboring state will be a surprise.)

Take a cab to a hotel where you've booked a suite filled with flowers and champagne. Order dinner from room service, and spend the weekend getting to know each other all over again.

Log Cabin Anniversary

Get away from it all at a secluded cabin in the country. Whether it's near a lake, by the ocean, or high atop a mountain meadow, time shared in a cabin is certain to bring the two of you closer together.

Several weeks before your anniversary, make arrangements to spend a weekend in a remote hideaway. When the weekend arrives, pack a cooler full of food and a suitcase full of casual clothes and leave the world behind.

Build a fire in the fireplace when you arrive. Cuddle up together on the floor and have a relaxing drink as you watch the flames dance over the logs.

Take advantage of the outdoor activities in the area. Walk hand-in-hand down a country lane. Pick a bouquet of wild daisies. Watch butterflies sip nectar from mauve-colored milkweed blossoms.

If you're staying near a lake, take a canoe, rowboat, or sailboat out for a quiet tour of the lake. Watch the loons and the herons fish. Cast a line out yourself — you may catch your supper!

If you're near the ocean, climb the boulders along the shore. Look for sea urchins and starfish in tide pools. Listen to the waves as they break on the shore.

In the mountains, look for the flash of brook trout as they swim in bubbling streams. Pause to watch an eagle soar far overhead. Take a closer look at tiny mountain wildflowers.

If the weather turns inclement, stay indoors and play a game of checkers. Curl up together and take turns reading aloud. Talk, talk, talk.

If your anniversary occurs in winter, dress warmly and get outdoors. Rediscover the joy of sledding down a snowy hill, or skating on a frozen lake. Or try something new, such as snowshoeing or cross-country skiing.

When you're cold, return to the warmth of your cabin. Build up the fire. Sip hot cocoa or mulled cider as you snuggle together under a blanket. Bake a couple of potatoes in the ashes in the hearth, and broil some thick steaks over the coals.

When the weekend's over (and all too soon, it will be), make a vow to do it all again — next anniversary!

Love in the Morning

If you and your mate are tennis enthusiasts, why not celebrate your anniversary with an early morning tennis match?

Whether it's indoor tennis or out in the open air, make sure you have the court you want. Book court time well in advance of the big day.

Play hard, but play for fun. This isn't a grudge match between Ivan Lendl and Chris Evert Lloyd.

After the match, take a quick shower, then head to your favorite restaurant for breakfast. Treat yourself royally with a Belgian waffle piled high with strawberries and whipped cream, or French toast dusted with powdered sugar and lemon sauce drizzled over the top.

As you sip a second cup of coffee, casually present your anniversary gifts to each other—lessons with a tennis pro, matching tennis rackets, or a diamond tennis bracelet, perhaps?

If tennis isn't your game, perhaps golf is. Teeing off on the front nine on a fine, sunny morning is a lovely way to begin another year of married life.

Take your time negotiating the sand traps and water hazards. Let others play through — you've got all the time in the world. When you finish the front nine, stop at the clubhouse for a hearty breakfast of bacon, eggs and hash brown potatoes — you'll wear it off on the back nine!

Before you head out for the next tee, pause to give each other your gifts — a new putter or five-wood, a crying towel, or, if you're really feeling extravagant, a new electric golf cart!

Luxurious Limo Ride _____

Living in the lap of luxury is a privilege given only to a few. At best, we can get a taste of it now and then. Let your wedding anniversary be one of those times!

Hire a limousine to take you out on the town (or around it). Many limo companies offer two- and three-hour tours complete with stereo music, television, champagne, and hors d'oeuvres for a fixed price. You can arrange to have the limo filled with roses or balloons. You can take a driving tour to scenic places around the city, hit some of the area's hot night spots, or travel nowhere in particular. Or you can wind up your limo ride at a local hotel, where a honeymoon suite awaits you.

Moonlight on Horseback _____

Are you and your partner horse-lovers? A night-time ride can go a long way to inspire a little romance.

Choose an evening near your anniversary when the moon is full. If you don't own your own horses, rent a pair from a local riding stable. Pack your saddlebags with the fixings for a moonlight picnic — sausage and cheese, fancy crackers, a bottle of wine, maybe some caviar, if you're so inclined. Since it's your anniversary, give the horses a treat, too. Take along some carrots or apples for them to munch on while you hold your little picnic.

Then amble down the trail, traveling single file when you need to, and riding abreast and holding hands when the trail (and the horses) allow. You may come across a great meadow. Give the horses their head and race under the moonlight. Or perhaps you'll reach a lake or the ocean. Run the horses through the water, and kick up some spray as you play in the waves.

Stop at a pretty little spot and have your picnic. If you've brought along a guitar or harmonica, sing love songs to each other (who cares if your singing is slightly off-key?). Then ride slowly home again, happy in the knowledge that you're traveling the same trail — together.

Movie Date _____

Going out to a movie may not sound like much, but have you

checked the price of first-run movie tickets lately? Throw in dinner beforehand, and snacks at the theatre, and you've got the ingredients of a major night out!

Check your local newspaper for listings of movies being shown near you. If you live near a college or university, a theatre near campus may be running a foreign film festival or a retrospective on French film noir movies. Perhaps there's an action flick or a romantic comedy playing downtown. Or maybe you're up for some Disney animation. Whatever you choose, make sure it's a movie both of you want to see.

Begin your date with an intimate dinner in a cozy little restaurant near the theatre. Or view the movie first, then stop off for pizza or an ice cream soda afterward.

When you get to the theatre, splurge on the biggest tub of hot, buttered popcorn the concessionaire offers. Buy some soft drinks to go with it. If you really feel like a kid with a ten-dollar bill, buy licorice, Junior Mints™, or Jujubes™ to round out your movie "meal."

Find your seats, then cuddle up close to each other as the lights go down. Put that big tub of popcorn between you and enjoy!

Riverboat Romance

Does chug-chugging slowly down a moonlit river aboard a stern-wheeler conjure up images of romance for you and your mate. If so, book an anniversary cruise!

Although the Mississippi River could be considered the national headquarters for packet boats, many other rivers, including the St. Croix and the Illinois, also have riverboat tours.

In addition to your choice of river, you can also choose the length of your cruise, from a two-hour dinner excursion to a two-week journey from Minneapolis-St. Paul to New Orleans (or vice versa).

Many states have either authorized riverboat gambling or are considering doing so. Riverboat trips featuring casinos, dinner and entertainment can be had in many spots along the Mississippi.

Whatever location you choose, you'll enjoy watching the

scenery slide by as the paddle wheel sends sprays of diamonds toward the sunset. You can wander the decks or sit on benches in front of the pilothouse. Or you can have a quiet drink in the stateroom below.

If you live in the desert Southwest, don't despair. Many resorts, most notably in Scottsdale, Arizona, and Palm Springs, California, offer gondola rides on nearby lakes.

For an hour or so, you can partake of the luxury of an authentic Venetian gondola, complete with a costumed gondolier, violinist, and wine. As dusk settles around you, you'll feel the romance of old Venice as you make stately progress around the lake. Chances are, you'll feel like stealing a kiss. Go ahead. The gondolier's trained not to look.

Romantic VCR Retreat _____

An evening at home can be just the ticket for a busy, two-career couple. And what better way to put a little romance into your night than a romantic movie?

If you can, leave work a little early on this special day. Stop on your way home and buy a big bouquet of flowers for the table. Switch on the stereo as you prepare a light supper together. One of you can toss the salad while the other whips up an omelet filled with all of your favorite ingredients — mushrooms, green peppers, cheese, ham, perhaps fresh tomatoes, too.

Turn the lights down low and light a candle or two to dine by. Share a favorite wine with your meal. Clear away the dishes, and give each other your presents.

Then retreat to your bedroom, pop a cassette into the VCR, and snuggle together in bed, propped up by piles of pillows.

Here's a partial list of movies known for their tender and romantic moments:

An Affair to Remember — Cary Grant and Deborah Kerr

An Officer and a Gentleman — Richard Gere and Debra Winger

Camelot — Richard Harris and Vanessa Redgrave

Camille — Greta Garbo and Robert Taylor

Casablanca — Humphrey Bogart and Ingrid Bergman

Desk Set — Spencer Tracy and Katharine Hepburn

Doctor Zhivago — Omar Sharif and Julie Christie

For Me and My Gal — Judy Garland and Gene Kelly

The French Lieutenant's Woman — Meryl Streep and Jeremy Irons

Ghost — Patrick Swayze and Demi Moore

The Ghost and Mrs. Muir — Gene Tierney and Rex Harrison

Gone With the Wind — Clark Gable and Vivien Leigh

Holiday Inn — Bing Crosby, Fred Astaire, and Marjorie Reynolds

It Happened One Night — Clark Gable and Claudette Colbert

Ivanhoe — Elizabeth Taylor and Robert Taylor

Jane Eyre — Zelah Clarke and Timothy Dalton

The King and I — Yul Brynner and Deborah Kerr

Love Story — Ryan O'Neal and Ali MacGraw

The Music Man — Robert Preston and Shirley Jones

Stormy Weather — Lena Horne and Cab Calloway

The Way We Were — Barbra Streisand and Robert Redford

West Side Story — Natalie Wood and Richard Beymer

The Wind and the Lion — Sean Connery and Candice Bergman

White Christmas — Bing Crosby, Danny Kaye, and Rosemary Clooney

Second Honeymoon

Did you go to a particularly romantic destination on your honeymoon? Visit it again on your anniversary! In fact, you can re-create your entire honeymoon — without the wedding-night jitters!

Leave at the same time of day, and drive the same highways. Eat at the same restaurants, stay in the same bed-and-breakfast establishment, walk the same paths. Visit the same antique shops, only this time, purchase that lamp you couldn't afford when you were newlyweds. Feel the same awe you felt the first time you saw Niagara Falls together.

Find an intimate moment to re-read your old love letters. Or better yet, write new ones. You may be surprised to find out how hotly the flames of love still burn!

Silent Celebration _____

Take inspiration from the old silent movies. Grab your camcorder and film a silent romance of your own.

Dig up some frivolous, romantic-looking costumes at your nearest Salvation Army or Goodwill store. If you like, put heavy circles of dark makeup around your eyes á la Theda Bara or Rudolph Valentino. Then pop a fresh videocassette into your camera and go to a nearby park.

Set the camera on a tripod, then stage a boy-girl meeting where the girl walks by and drops a hanky. Act shy. Glance coyly at the camera. Bat your eyes at each other. Use wild, exaggerated gestures. Take turns filming each other on the swings. If your camera has variable speed settings, film the action at a slower speed. When the tape is played back, you'll have the jerky motions so well associated with the early days of Hollywood filmmaking.

Go to a local rail yard and film train engines moving toward you. Then find an *unused* section of track and loosely tie the "heroine" down to it. Set the camera on a tripod again and film the rescue. When the rescue is complete, film a joyful kiss or two, followed by a graceful swoon.

After you've used up all your film (shoot plenty, film is cheap!), take it to an editing studio. For approximately $100 an hour (depending on where you live, and the studio's facilities), you can give your film a more professional touch. You can edit in subtitles, and special effects. The soundtrack can be erased, and old-fashioned, melodramatic piano music dubbed over the pictures. You'll have a terrific finished product, and an anniversary keepsake you can view over and over again.

Sports Night Out _____

Do you and your mate enjoy cheering on your local college football team? Are you avid hockey fans? Or maybe an afternoon of baseball is more your style. Make a date to watch the sport of your choice on your anniversary.

Precede the event with a tailgate picnic out of the trunk of your car. Tailgating can be as plain or as fancy as you care to make it, from a simple hotdog on a roasting fork, to a seven-course meal complete with wine and a white tablecloth (allow for extra time, of course!). If tailgating is not permitted (or the weather won't cooperate), hold a pre-game "warm-up" at a cozy restaurant near the arena or stadium.

Inside the arena itself, go a little crazy. Buy some pompoms or a pennant — or a crazy hat. Yell, and have a good time cheering your team on to victory.

Perhaps auto racing or horse racing is your sport. If so, consider taking a trip on your anniversary to a special race — the Indy 500, perhaps or the Kentucky Derby or the Preakness. Place some bets just for fun (you may even want to bet against each other).

Whether it's pro basketball or amateur ski-jumping, there's sure to be a sport that will thrill and amuse you. Who knows? Maybe your team will win the World Series on your anniversary!

Suites for the Sweet

A hotel suite can provide a very romantic backdrop for an anniversary celebration. Once reserved for the very rich, suites are now available to the general public through a variety of package deals.

Some hotels advertise their suite packages only before Valentine's Day. If you'd like to treat your sweetheart to a romantic rendezvous in August, don't despair. Talk with the hotel management and ask if you can book a suite for your anniversary, and "by the way, would you be willing to include the amenities you offered in your Valentine's promotion — for the same price?" Chances are, you'll be able to work out a satisfactory arrangement.

Suite packages vary from hotel to hotel. Some offer a night's lodging and complimentary drink tickets. Others include champagne and roses upon arrival. Others offer champagne, roses, chocolates on your pillow, and dinner for two. Still others transport you to another world where you can stay in your choice of a treehouse, an igloo, a Roman temple, or a space capsule.

Nor do the possibilities end there. Imagine having a French picnic in your guest room. Or sharing a bubble bath in a heart-shaped whirlpool. Or sleeping in a bed made from a Venetian gondola.

You'll come home saying, "How suite it is!"

Tandem Treat

East Side, West Side, a bicycle built for two is still a great way to get around town — and spend a delightful afternoon with a loved one.

Not many people can afford to own one, but many bike dealers have tandems you can rent on a daily basis. What's more, a bicycle built for two doesn't require any fancy equipment — although a pair of safety helmets (*His* and *Hers*?) is a good idea.

In many rural areas, bike paths have been carved out of old railroad rights-of-way. Whether you follow a city parkway or travel the countryside, plan a route with a particular scenic destination in mind, such as a park, lake, or overlook.

Fill a backpack with fruit and sandwiches. Take along plenty of cold water (biking is thirsty work!).

Beat summer heat by starting out early in the day. In the fall or spring, bring along light jackets you toss on or slip off at a moment's notice. Slip a disposable camera into a jacket pocket to capture memories on the spot.

When you return home, slip into your spa or hot tub to relieve tired muscles and ward off the first signs of saddle soreness. Sip a favorite beverage as you soak in the warm water, and plan your next anniversary's outing.

A Way to a Man's (or Woman's!) Heart

It's not uncommon to find both husband and wife in the kitchen these days. In fact, cozy conversations while the white sauce is simmering is a good way to keep the romantic fire going as well!

The perfect anniversary gift for a cooking couple to give each other is lessons at a local cooking school. Whether the subject is *nouvelle cuisine* or the secrets of Polish peasant cooking, spending more time in the kitchen together is sure to be a delight.

You'll have fun, too, giving each other the latest in a never-ending stream of new kitchen gadgets, from French-designed electronic apple peelers to automatic bread-making machines. And, of course, you'll have to have matching chef's hats and aprons!

Bon appetit!

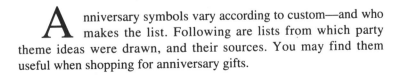

Anniversary
Symbols

A nniversary symbols vary according to custom—and who makes the list. Following are lists from which party theme ideas were drawn, and their sources. You may find them useful when shopping for anniversary gifts.

Source: Hallmark Cards

	Traditional	**Modern**
First	paper	clocks
Second	cotton	china
Third	leather/linen	crystal/glass
Fourth	fruit/flowers/books	appliances
Fifth	wood	silverware
Sixth	candy/iron	wood
Seventh	wool/copper/brass	desk sets
Eighth	bronze/pottery	linens/laces
Ninth	pottery/willow	leather
Tenth	tin/aluminum	diamond jewelry
Eleventh	steel	fashion jewelry
Twelfth	silk/linen	pearls
Thirteenth	lace	textiles/furs
Fourteenth	ivory	gold jewelry
Fifteenth	crystal	watches
Twentieth	china	platinum
Twenty-fifth	silver	silver
Thirtieth	pearl	diamond
Thirty-fifth	coral	jade
Fortieth	ruby	ruby
Forty-fifth	sapphire/alexandrite	sapphire
Fiftieth	gold	gold
Fifty-fifth	emerald	emerald
Sixtieth	diamond/platinum	diamond
Seventy-fifth	diamond	diamond

Source: Anniversary Gift List,
American Gem Society

Anniversary Gems and Jewelry

First	gold jewelry
Second	garnet (all colors)
Third	pearls
Fourth	blue topaz
Fifth	sapphire (all colors)
Sixth	amethyst
Seventh	onyx
Eighth	tourmaline (all colors)
Ninth	lapis
Tenth	diamond jewelry
Eleventh	turquoise
Twelfth	jade
Thirteenth	citrine
Fourteenth	opal
Fifteenth	ruby
Sixteenth	peridot
Seventeenth	watches
Eighteenth	cat's eye
Nineteenth	aquamarine
Twentieth	emeralds
Twenty-First	iolite
Twenty-Second	spinel (all colors)
Twenty-third	imperial topaz
Twenty-fourth	Tarzanite
Twenty-fifth	silver jubilee
Thirtieth	pearl jubilee
Thirty-fifth	emerald
Fortieth	ruby

Forty-fifth	sapphire
Fiftieth	golden jubilee
Fifty-fifth	alexandrite
Sixtieth	diamond jubilee

Here's a slightly offbeat list from Frosig's 1983 gift catalog. (Frosig's is a Danish china firm.)

First	paper
Second	cotton
Third	leather
Fourth	flowers
Fifth	wood
Sixth	sugar
Seventh	wool
Eighth	bronze
Ninth	willow
Tenth	pewter
Eleventh	steel
Twelfth	silk
Twelfth and One-half	copper
Thirteenth	lace
Fourteenth	ivory
Fifteenth	crystal
Twentieth	porcelain
Twenty-fifth	silver
Thirtieth	pearl
Thirty-fifth	coral
Fortieth	ruby
Forty-fifth	sapphire
Fiftieth	gold

Fifty-fifth	emerald
Sixtieth	diamond
Sixty-fifth	crown diamond
Seventieth	iron
Seventy-fifth	atom

Source: A Brief Dictionary of American Superstitions,
by
Vergilius Ferm, The Philosophical Library, 1959.

Gem Sources:

A list of not-so-common anniversary symbols

Thirteenth	moonstone
Fourteenth	moss Agate
Fifteenth	rock/crystal/glass
Sixteenth	topaz/topaz-quartz
Seventeenth	amethyst
Eighteenth	garnet
Nineteenth	hyacinth zircon
Twenty-third	sapphire
Twenty-sixth	star sapphire, blue
Thirty-ninth	cat's eye
Fifty-second	star sapphire, ruby
Sixty-fifth	star sapphire, gray
Sixty-seventh	star sapphire, purple

Flowers That Say "I Love You"

F lowers have long been thought to have a language of their
own. In the mid-Nineteenth Century, lovers used flowers
to convey their feelings.

In 1884, artist Kate Greenaway published an illustrated book
called the *Language of Flowers* which listed flowers and their
various messages. Another version of the book appeared in 1913,
when an unknown author published a small book as a gift to his wife
on their golden wedding anniversary. The following list of "love"
flowers and their meanings is taken from these two books, and from
lists provided by the Society of American Florists. Use them to send
your own special messages of love.

"Love Flowers" _____

Acacia, rose or white	Elegance
Acacia, yellow	Secret love
Almond, flowering	Hope
Alyssum, sweet	Worth beyond beauty
Amaranth, globe	Unfading love
Amaryllis	Splendid beauty
Ambrosia	Love returned
American Linden	Matrimony
Angelica	Inspiration, magic
Apple	Temptation
Apple blossom	Preference
Arum	Ardor
Bay Tree	Glory
Bellflower, pyramidal	Constancy
Betony	Surprise
Bluebell	Constancy
Borus Henricus	Goodness
Bridal rose	Happy love
Bundle of Reeds, with their panicles	Music
Cactus	Warmth
Calceolaria	I offer you my fortune
Calla Ethiopica	Magnificent beauty
Camellia Japonica, white	Perfected loveliness
Catchfly, red	Youthful love
Cedar leaf	I live for thee
Celandine, lesser	Joys to come
Chickweed	Rendezvous
China aster, double	I partake of your sentiments

China rose	Beauty always new
Chrysanthemum, red	I love
Chrysanthemum, white	Truth
Cineraria	Always delightful
Clematis	Mental beauty
Clover, four-leaved	Be mine
Clover, white	Think of me
Coreopsis Arkansa	Love at first sight
Coreopsis	Always cheerful
Corn	Riches
Cowslip, American	Divine Beauty
Cuckoo plant	Ardor
Cudweed, American	Unceasing remembrance
Daffodil	Regard
Daisy, garden	I share your sentiments
Daisy, party-colored	Beauty
Dittany of Crete, white	Passion
Escholzia	Do not refuse me
Everlasting Pea	Lasting pleasure
Fennel	Worth all praise, strength
Fern	Fascination
Filbert	Reconciliation
Fleur-de-Lis	Flame, I burn
Forget-me-not	True love, forget me not
French Honeysuckle	Rustic beauty
Garden Chervil	Sincerity
Garden Ranunculus	You are rich in attractions
Garden Sage	Esteem
Garland of Roses	Reward of virtue
Geranium, Ivy	Bridal flower
Geranium, Rose-scented	Preference
Gillyflower	Bonds of affection

Glory Flower	Glorious beauty
Gorse	Love for all seasons
Hawthorn	Hope
Hazel	Reconciliation
Heliotrope	Devotion, faithfulness
Hepatica	Confidence
Holly herb	Enchantment
Honey Flower	Love, sweet and secret
Honeysuckle	Generous and devoted affection
Indian jasmine (Ipomoea)	Attachment
Indian pink (double)	Always lovely
Iris (German)	Flame
Ivy	Fidelity, marriage
Jasmine, Cape	Transport of joy
Jasmine, Spanish	Sensuality
Jasmine, yellow	Grace and elegance
Justicia	The perfection of female loveliness
Lady's slipper	Win me
Laurel	Glory
Lemon blossoms	Fidelity in love
Lilac, purple	First emotions of love
Lily of the valley	Return of happiness
Lily, white	Purity, sweetness
Linden or lime trees	Conjugal love
Locust tree (green)	Affection beyond the grave
Lucern	Life
Mallow, Syrian	Consumed by love
Mallow, Venetian	Delicate beauty
Marjoram	Blushes
Mezereon	Desire to please
Mignonette	Your qualities surpass your charms
Mimosa (sensitive plant)	Sensitiveness

Mint	Virtue
Mossy saxifrage	Affection
Mudwort	Tranquillity
Mugwort	Happiness
Myrrh	Gladness
Myrtle	Love
Olive	Peace
Orange blossoms	Your purity equals your loveliness
Orange flowers	Bridal festivities
Orange tree	Generosity
Peach blossom	I am your captive
Peach	Your qualities, like your charms, are unequaled
Pear Tree	Comfort
Pear	Affection
Peony	Bashfulness
Peppermint	Warmth of feeling
Peruvian heliotrope	Devotion
Petunia	Your presence soothes me
Pheasant's eye	Remembrance
Phlox	Unanimity
Pineapple	You are perfect
Pink, carnation	Woman's love
Pink, mountain	Aspiring
Pink, red, double	Pure and ardent love
Pink, single	Pure love
Rose, Austrian	Thou art all that is lovely
Rose, Bridal	Happy love
Rose, Burgundy	Unconscious beauty
Rose, cabbage	Ambassador of love
Rose, China	Beauty always new
Rose, daily	Thy smile I aspire to

Rose, full-blown, placed over two buds	Secrecy
Rose, Maiden blush	If you love me, you will find me
Rose, Multiflora	Grace
Rose, musk, cluster	Charming
Rose, single	Simplicity
Rose, thornless	Early attachment
Rose, white and red together	Unity
Rose, white	I am worthy of you
Rosebud, Moss	Confession of love
Rosebud, red	Pure and lovely
Rosebud, white	Girlhood
Rose	Love
Roses, crown of	Reward of virtue
Scarlet Lychnis	Sunbeaming eyes
Snowdrop	Hope
Sorrel, wood	Joy
Sorrel	Affection
Spearmint	Warmth of sentiment
Speedwell	Female fidelity
Spindletree	Your charms are engraved upon my heart
Star of Bethlehem	Purity
Stock	Lasting beauty
Stonecrop	Tranquillity
Straw, whole	Union
Strawberry tree	Esteem and love
Sumach, Venice	Splendor, intellectual excellence
Sunflower, dwarf	Adoration
Sweet Pea	Delicate pleasures
Sweet William	Gallantry
Trillium pictum	Modest beauty

Tulip, red	Declaration of love
Tulip, variegated	Beautiful eyes
Venus' Car	Fly with me
Veronica	Fidelity
Vervain	Enchantment
Vine	Intoxication
Violet, blue	Faithfulness
Violet, sweet	Watchfulness
Violet, yellow	Rural happiness
Water lily	Purity of heart

Index

A

American West, 45 – 46
Anniversary High Tea, 124
Anniversary preparations at
    your wedding, 18 – 19
Anniversary Symbols,
    139 – 143
Amethyst (Seventeenth)
    Anniversary, 80 – 81
gift suggestions for, 81
Aquamarine (Nineteenth)
    Anniversary, 83 – 84
gift suggestions for, 84
Arabian Nights Silken
    Fantasy, 68 – 69
Archaeological Dig, 55 – 56
Artful Afternoon, 124 – 125
Attendants' Candlelight
    Dinner, 37 – 38
Australian Outback Barbecue,
    72 – 74

B

Brass (Seventh) Anniversary,
    57 – 59
gift suggestions for, 59
Bronze (Eighth) Anniversary,
    59 – 61
gift suggestions for, 60 – 61
Bronze Brunch, 60
Business . . . or Pleasure?, 125

C

Candy (Sixth) Anniversary,
    54 – 55
gift suggestions for, 56 – 57
Card "Showers," 25

Celebrating your anniversary,
    17 – 32
Champagne Balloon Flight,
    125 – 126
China (Twentieth) Anniver-
    sary, 84 – 87
gift suggestions for, 86 – 87
Chinese Garden Party, 86
Cinderella's Crystal Ball,
    74 – 76
Classic Camp-out, 126 – 127
"Come as You Were 25 Years
    Ago" Party, 91 – 92
Copper (Seventh) Anniver-
    sary, 57 –59
gift suggestions for, 58 – 59
Coral (Thirty-fifth) Anniver-
    sary, 100 – 102
gift suggestions for,
    101 – 102
Cotton Bowl Anniversary,
    42 – 43
Cotton (Second) Anniversary,
    42 – 45
gift suggestions for, 44 – 45
Crystal (Fifteenth) Anniver-
    sary, 74 – 76
gift suggestions for, 75 – 76

D

Dancing in the Dark,
    127 – 128
Decorations, 27 – 28
Diamond (Sixtieth) Anniver-
    sary, 118 – 119
gift suggestions for, 119
Dinner Theatre Date, 128

E

Eighteenth Anniversary
(Garnet), 81 – 83
gift suggestions for, 82 – 83
Eighth Anniversary (Bronze),
59 – 61
gift suggestions for, 60 – 61
Eleventh Anniversary (Steel),
66 – 67
gift suggestions for, 67
Emerald City Party, 116 – 117
Emerald (Fifty-fifth) Anniversary, 116 – 118
gift suggestions for,
117 – 118
Ethnic Anniversary
Celebration, 92 – 93
Etiquette, 19 – 23

F

Fifteenth Anniversary
(Crystal), 74 – 76
gift suggestions for, 75 – 76
"Fifties" Fiftieth Anniversary,
111 – 112
Fiftieth Anniversary (Gold),
107 – 113
gift suggestions for, 112 –
113
Fiftieth Family Reunion,
109 – 111
Fifty-fifth Anniversary
(Emerald), 116 – 117
gift suggestions for,
117 – 118
First Anniversary (Paper),
33 – 40
gift suggestions for, 39 – 40
Floral Fantasy, 48 – 49

Flower (Fourth) Anniversary,
47 – 49
gift suggestions for, 49
Flowers,
as decorations, 28, 48
as celebration theme,
48 – 49
That Say "I Love You",
145 – 151
Forgetful spouse, reminding,
31 – 32
Fortieth Anniversary (Ruby),
102 – 104
gift suggestions for, 104
Forty-fifth Anniversary
(Sapphire), 104 – 106
gift suggestions for, 106
Fourteenth Anniversary
(Opal), 72 – 74
gift suggestions for, 73 – 74
Fourth Anniversary (Flower),
47 – 49
gift suggestions for, 49

G

Garnet (Eighteenth) Anniversary, 81 – 83
gift suggestions for, 82 – 83
Gifts, 23 – 26
monetary, 25
"No Gifts, Please", 24
suggestions, 39 – 40,
44 – 45, 46 – 47, 49,
51 – 52, 56 – 57, 58 – 59,
61, 62 – 63, 64 –65, 68,
70, 72 – 73, 74 – 75,
76 – 77, 80, 82, 83 – 84,
85, 87 – 88, 95 – 96, 99,
102, 104, 106, 112 – 113,
116 – 117, 118, 121, 130

to anniversary couple, 24
to each other, 23 – 24
Golden Anniversary Gala,
    108 – 109
Golden (Fiftieth) Anniversary,
    107 – 113
  gift suggestions for,
    112 – 113
Great Couples, 100 – 101
Great Dates: Anniversary
    Celebrations for the Two
    of You, 122 – 138
Grecian Holiday, 80 – 81

H
Harlem Cotton Club Anniver-
    sary Party, 43 – 44
Hawaiian Sapphire Celebra-
    tion, 104 – 106

I
Invitations, 20 – 23
Iron (Sixth) Anniversary,
    54 – 55
  gift suggestions for, 56 – 57

J
Jamaican Steel Drum Party,
    66 – 67

K
Kidnaped Bride/Groom,
    128 – 129

L
Lace (Thirteenth) Anniver-
    sary, 70 – 72
  gift suggestions for, 71 – 72

Leather (Third) Anniversary,
    45 – 47
  gift suggestions for, 46 – 47
Linen (Twelfth) Anniversary,
    68 – 69
  gift suggestions for, 69
Log Cabin Anniversary,
    129 – 130
Love in the Morning,
    130 – 131
Luxurious Limo Ride, 131

M
Medieval Madness, 98 – 99
"money tree," 25, 90
Moonlight on Horseback, 131
Moonstone (Thirteenth) Anni-
    versary, 70 – 72
  gift suggestions for, 71 – 72
Movie Date, 131 – 132
Music
  at anniversaries, 28 – 29
  suggestions, 28 – 29, 63, 73,
    78, 91 – 92, 103 – 104,
    105, 112

N
Nineteenth (Aquamarine)
    Anniversary, 83 – 84
  gift suggestions for, 84
Ninth (Pottery, Willow) Anni-
    versary, 61 – 63

O
Opal (Fourteenth) Anniver-
    sary, 72 – 74
  gift suggestion for, 73 – 74

P

Party activities, 26 – 27
Paper Chase, 36
Paper (First) Anniversary,
 33 – 40
 gift suggestions for, 39 – 40
Pearl (Thirtieth) Anniversary,
 98 – 99
 gift suggestions for, 99
Photographs,
 as gifts, 30, 110 – 111, 118,
 137
 at anniversary, 29 – 30, 121
Platinum Anniversary Party,
 120 – 122
Platinum (Seventy-fifth) Anniversary, 120 – 121
 gift suggestions for, 122
Pottery (Ninth) Anniversary,
 61 – 63
 gift suggestions for, 62 – 63
Pottery Picnic, 61 – 62
Programs, printed, 29
Publicity, 30 – 31

R

Reaffirmation, 23
 invitation for, 23
 Twenty-fifth Reaffirmation,
 94 – 95
Reassessment Weekend, 58
Receiving line, 27, 90, 109
Riverboat Romance,
 132 – 133
Roaring Twenties Twentieth,
 85 – 86
Romantic Paper Picnic,
 34 – 35
Romantic VCR Retreat,
 133 – 134

Ruby (Fortieth) Anniversary,
 102 – 104
 gift suggestions for, 104
Ruby-colored Fortieth,
 102 – 104

S

Sapphire (Forty-fifth) Anniversary, 104 – 106
 gift suggestions for, 106
Seashore Holiday, 83 – 84
Second (Cotton) Anniversary,
 42 – 45
 gift suggestions for, 44 – 45
Second Honeymoon,
 134 – 135
Seventeenth (Amethyst) Anniversary, 80 – 81
 gift suggestions for, 81
Seventh (Wool, Copper,
 Brass) Anniversary,
 57 – 59
 gift suggestions for, 58 – 59
Seventy-fifth (Platinum) Anniversary, 120 – 122
 gift suggestions for, 122
Silent Celebration, 135
Silk (Twelfth) Anniversary,
 68 – 69
 gift suggestions for, 69
Silver (Twenty-fifth) Anniversary, 89 – 96
 gift suggestions for, 95 – 96
Sixteenth (Topaz) Anniversary, 78 – 79
 gift suggestions for, 79
Sixth (Candy, Iron) Anniversary, 54 – 57
 gift suggestions for, 56 – 57

Sixtieth (Diamond) Anniversary, 118 – 119
gift suggestions for, 119
Sixtieth Diamond Jubilee, 118 – 119
South American Sampler, 78 – 79
Sports Night Out, 135 – 136
Steel (Eleventh) Anniversary, 66 – 67
gift suggestions for, 67
Suites for the Sweet, 136 – 137
Sweet Sixth, 54 – 55

T

Tandem Treat, 137
Tenth (Tin) Anniversary, 63 – 64
gift suggestions for, 64
Tent Party, 63 – 64
Timely Celebration, 38 – 39
Tin (Tenth) Anniversary, 63 – 64
gift suggestions for, 64
Thank-yous, 25 – 26
Third (Leather) Anniversary, 45 – 47
gift suggestions for, 46 – 47
Thirteenth (Lace, Moonstone) Anniversary, 70 – 72
gift suggestions for, 71 – 72
Thirtieth (Pearl) Anniversary, 98 – 99
gift suggestions for, 99
Thirty-fifth (Coral) Anniversary, 100 – 102
gift suggestions for, 102
Toasts, 27, 38, 51, 75, 99, 101, 117, 121

Topaz (Sixteenth) Anniversary, 78 – 79
gift suggestions for, 79
Traditional Silver Jubilee, 90 – 91
Tree-planting Ceremony, 50 – 51
Twelfth (Silk, Linen) Anniversary, 68 – 69
gift suggestions for, 69
Twentieth (China) Anniversary, 84 – 87
gift suggestions for, 86 – 87
Twenty-fifth (Silver) Anniversary, 89 – 96
gift suggestions for, 95 – 96
Twenty-fifth Reaffirmation, 94 – 95

V

Victorian Lace Breakfast in Bed, 70
Victorian Romance, 82
Videotape Viewing, 35 – 36

W

Way to a Man's (or Woman's) Heart!, 137 – 138
Widows and widowers, remembering, 32
Wilkie Collins Moonstone Murder Mystery Party, 71 – 72
Willow (Ninth) Anniversary, 61 – 63
gift suggestions for, 62 – 63
Wool (Seventh) Anniversary, 57 – 59
gift suggestions for, 58 – 59

❦

About the Author

Cynthia Lueck Sowden is a native of Minneapolis, Minnesota. A graduate of the University of Minnesota School of Journalism and Mass Communications, she worked for several years in public relations and advertising before becoming a freelance writer and editor in 1984. "An Anniversary to Remember" is her second book. Her first, "Wedding Occasions," was published by Brighton Publications in 1990.

Sowden and her husband, Ralph, have been married since 1979. They have a daughter, Elizabeth.

Available from Brighton Publications, Inc.

Reunions for Fun-Loving Families by Nancy Funke Bagle

Folding Table Napkins by Sharon Dlugosch

Table Setting Guide by Sharon Dlugosch

Tabletop Vignettes by Sharon Dlugosch

Games for Party Fun by Sharon Dlugosch

Christmas Party Celebrations: 71 New and Exciting Party Plans for Holiday Fun by Denise Distel Dytrych

Romantic At-Home Dinners: Sneaky Strategies for Couples with Kids by Nan Booth/Gary Fischler

Kid-Tastic Birthday Parties: The Complete Party Planner for Today's Kids by Jane Chase

Baby Shower Fun by Sharon Dlugosch

Games for Baby Shower Fun by Sharon Dlugosch

Wedding Occasions: 101 New Party Themes for Wedding Showers, Rehearsal Dinners, Engagement Parties, and More! by Cynthia Lueck Sowden

Games for Wedding Shower Fun by Sharon Dlugosch, Florence Nelson

Wedding Plans: 50 Unique Themes for the Wedding of Your Dreams by Sharon Dlugosch

Wedding Hints & Reminders by Sharon Dlugosch

Dream Weddings Do Come True: How to Plan a Stress-Free Wedding by Cynthia Kreuger

Don't Slurp Your Soup: A Basic Guide to Business Etiquette by Elizabeth Craig

Hit the Ground Running: Communicate Your Way to Business Success by Cynthia Kreuger

Installation Ceremonies for Every Group: 26 Memorable Ways to Install New Officers by Pat Hines

Meeting Room Games: Getting Things Done in Committees by Nan Booth

These books are available in selected stores. If you need help finding them in your area, send a self-addressed, stamped, business-size envelope and request ordering information from:

Brighton Publications, Inc.
P.O. Box 120706
St. Paul, MN 55112-0706

call: 1-800-536-BOOK (2665)

web: http://www.partybooks.com